Whose
Story
Is This?

Also Available from Haymarket Books by Rebecca Solnit

Call Them by Their True Names: American Crises (and Essays)

Cinderella Liberator, illustrated by Arthur Rackham

Hope in the Dark: Untold Histories, Wild Possibilities

Los hombres me explican cosas

Men Explain Things to Me

The Mother of All Questions

"City of Women" map, created with Joshua Jelly-Schapiro

Whose Story Is This?

Old Conflicts, New Chapters

Rebecca Solnit

Haymarket Books
Chicago, Illinois

Published in 2019 by
Haymarket Books
P.O. Box 180165
Chicago, IL 60618
773-583-7884
www.haymarketbooks.org
info@haymarketbooks.org

ISBN: 978-1-64259-172-9

Distributed to the trade in the US through Consortium Book Sales and
Distribution (www.cbsd.com) and internationally through Ingram Publisher Services International (www.ingramcontent.com).

This book was published with the generous support of Lannan Foundation
and Wallace Action Fund.

Special discounts are available for bulk purchases by organizations and
institutions. Please call 773-583-7884 or email info@haymarketbooks.org
for more information.

Cover design by Abby Weintraub. Interior maps courtesy of the US
Geological Survey.

Printed in the United States.

Library of Congress Cataloging-in-Publication data is available.

Contents

Cathedrals and Alarm Clocks

We are building something immense together that, though invisible and immaterial, is a structure, one we reside within—or, rather, many overlapping structures. They're assembled from ideas, visions and values emerging out of conversations, essays, editorials, arguments, slogans, social-media messages, books, protests, and demonstrations. About race, class, gender, sexuality; about nature, power, climate, the interconnectedness of all things; about compassion, generosity, collectivity, communion; about justice, equality, possibility. Though there are individual voices and people who got there first, these are collective projects that matter not when one person says something but when a million integrate it into how they see and act in the world. The *we* who inhabits those structures grows as what was once subversive or transgressive settles in as normal, as people outside the walls wake up one day inside them and forget they were ever anywhere else.

The consequences of these transformations are perhaps most important where they are most subtle. They remake the world, and they do so mostly by the accretion of small gestures and statements and the embracing of new visions of what can be and should be. The unknown becomes known, the outcasts come inside, the strange becomes ordinary. You can see changes to the ideas about whose rights matter and what is reasonable and who should decide, if you sit still enough and gather the evidence of transformations that happen by a million tiny steps before they result in a landmark legal decision or an election or some other shift that puts us in a place we've never been.

I have been watching this beautiful collective process of change unfold with particular intensity over the past several years—generated by the work of countless people separately and together, by the delegitimization of the past and the hope for a better future that lay behind the genesis of Occupy Wall Street (2011), Idle No More (2012), Black Lives Matter (2013), #MeToo (2017), and the new feminist surges and insurgencies, immigrant and trans rights movements, the Green New Deal (2018), and the growing power and reach of the climate movement. In the US, advocacy of universal healthcare, the elimination of the Electoral College, the end of the death penalty, and an energy revolution that leaves fossil fuels behind have gone from the margins to the center in recent years. A new clarity about how injustice works, from police murders to the endless excuses and victim-blaming for rape, lays bare the machinery of that injustice, makes it recognizable when it recurs, and that recognizability strips away the disguises of and excuses for the old ways.

My formative intellectual experience was, in the early 1990s, watching reactions against the celebration of the quincentennial of Columbus's arrival in the Americas and the rise in visibility and audibility of Native Americans that radically redefined this hemisphere's history and ideas about nature and culture. That was how I learned that culture matters, that it's the substructure of beliefs that shape politics, that change begins on the margins and in the shadows and grows toward the center, that the center is a place of arrival and rarely one of real generation, and that even the most foundational stories can be changed. But now I recognize it's not the margins, the place of beginnings, or the center, the place of arrival, but the pervasiveness that matters most.

We live inside ideas. Some are shelters, some are observatories, some are windowless prisons. We are leaving some behind and entering others. At its best, in recent years, this has been a collaborative process so swift and powerful that those paying closest attention can see the doors being framed, the towers arising, the spaces taking shape in which our thoughts will reside—and other structures being knocked down. Oppressions and exclusions so accepted they're nearly invisible become visible en route to becoming unacceptable, and other mores replace the old ones. Those who watch with care can see the structure expanding so that some of those who object or ridicule or fail to comprehend will, within a few years, not even question their lives inside those frameworks. Others try to stop these new edifices from arising; they succeed better with legislation than with imagination. That is, you can prevent women from having access to abortions more easily than you can prevent them from thinking they have the right to an abortion.

You can see change itself happening, if you watch carefully and keep track of what was versus what is. That's some of what I've tried to do over the years, in this book and others: to see change and understand how it works and how and where each of us has power within it. To recognize that we live in a transformative time, and that this process will continue beyond what we can now imagine. I've watched the arising of new ways of naming how women have been oppressed and erased, heard the insistence that the oppression and erasure will no longer be acceptable or invisible. Often, even things that impacted me most directly became clearer through this process, carried out by many of us together. I've seen many writers express versions of the same general principles, seen the ideas catch on, spread, become incorporated into conversations about what is and should be, and sometimes I've been one of those writers. To see it unfolding is exhilarating and sometimes awe-inspiring.

This is a time in which the power of words to introduce and justify and explain ideas matters, and that power is tangible in the changes at work. Forgetting is a problem; words matter, partly as a means to help us remember. When the cathedrals you build are invisible, made of perspectives and ideas, you forget you are inside them and that the ideas they consist of were, in fact, *made*, constructed by people who analyzed and argued and shifted our assumptions. They are the fruit of labor. Forgetting means a failure to recognize the power of the process and the fluidity of meanings and values.

I heard Gerard Baker talk recently. He's Mandan-Hidatsa, from the Fort Berthold reservation in North Dakota, and he spoke about his work in the national parks to change the way Native people were present, literally, as visitors and employees, as well as in structures, signs, language, and other representations. Immensely tall, enormously funny, a brilliant raconteur, he told us how he rose from doing janitorial work to being superintendent at two national monuments he'd told his family he'd never work at, Little Bighorn Battlefield (which was, until 1991, named Custer Battlefield National Monument) and Mount Rushmore. At both parks he changed what the place meant and whom it was for. At one he got death threats for doing so; some people intend to keep the old versions in place by violence.

Recalling what he said, remembering my own early 1990s re-education about Native American presences in the United States, contemplating the conversations we have now and those we don't, I wanted to yell at some of the people I run into, "If you think you're woke, it's because someone woke you up, so thank the human alarm clocks." It's easy now to assume that one's perspectives on race, gender, orientation, and the rest are signs of inherent virtue, but a lot of ideas currently in circulation are gifts that arrived recently, through the labors of others.

Remembering that people made these ideas, as surely as people made the buildings we live in and the roads we travel on, helps us remember that, first, change is possible, and second, it's our good luck to live in the wake of this change rather than asserting our superiority to those who came before the new structures, and maybe even to acknowledge that we have not arrived at a state of perfect enlightenment, because there is more change to come, more that we do not yet recognize that will be revealed. I have learned so much. I have so much to learn.

There's a beautiful passage Black Lives Matter cofounder Alicia Garza wrote in the wake of the 2016 election:

> This is a moment for all of us to remember who we were when we stepped into the movement—to remember the organizers who were patient with us, who disagreed with us and yet stayed connected, who smiled knowingly when our self-righteousness consumed us. Building a movement requires reaching out beyond the people who agree with you. I remember who I was before I gave my life to the movement. Someone was patient with me. Someone saw that I had something to contribute. Someone stuck with me. Someone did the work to increase my commitment. Someone taught me how to be accountable. Someone opened my eyes to the root causes of the problems we face. Someone pushed me to call forward my vision for the future. Someone trained me to bring other people who are looking for a movement into one.

Garza acknowledges that each of us had an education and implies that none of our educations is finished. At its best, at its most beautiful, this is a creative process. At its worst, it's policing by those who are inside aimed at those who are not. Sometimes they're not inside because they have not yet found the doorway or they hear condemnation rather than invitation issue from the doorstep. But people also forget that this is a historical process rather than ideas that have always been self-evident, and some have had more access to these ideas than others. I find now that most people forget the immense work done around race and gender and sexuality and prisons and power, and that it was, in fact, *work*—intellectual labor to reject the assumptions built into language, the forces that lift some of us up and push others down, to understand and describe the past and the present and propose new possibilities for the future.

Amnesia means that people forget the stunning scope of change in recent decades. That change is itself hopeful, as evidence that people considered marginal or powerless—scholars, activists, people speaking for and from within oppressed groups—have changed the world. For example, an unfortunate consequence of the relative success of what got called #MeToo has been to imagine that something began at that point. This obscures the extraordinary feminism of the five years before, including the work of campus anti-rape activists and the responses to the rape-torture-murder of Jyoti Singh in New Delhi and the Steubenville sexual assault case.

Even the surge of public response to those atrocities may obscure, as I wrote in one of the essays in this book, that the reason women's stories were able to be heard and generated consequences was because of what came before: the long, slow work of feminism to change consciousness and to put women—and men who regarded women as human beings endowed with inalienable rights and the capacity to say things that mattered—in positions of power. And the rise of new generations who were less bound by the old assumptions and denials. To change who tells the story, and who decides, is to change whose story this is.

The watershed called #MeToo in October 2017 was not that people spoke; it's that other people listened. Many had spoken up before—the victims of the gymnastics doctor, the victims of R. Kelly—some over and over, and their testimony was ignored or disregarded. So #MeToo was not the beginning of women speaking up, but of people listening, and even then—as we've seen in the case of Christine Blasey Ford, testifying against Supreme Court nominee Brett Kavanaugh—continuing to be silenced. Just as Gerard Baker did, for changing the story about the Battle of Little Bighorn, Blasey Ford received death threats. One measure of how much power these voices and stories have is how frantically others try to stop them.

The title essay of this anthology is about the struggle of new stories to be born, against the forces that prefer to shut them out or shout us down, against people who work hard at not hearing and not seeing. A far, far too common response to #MeToo has been to bemoan that men feel less comfortable in their workplaces, which springs first of all from a habit of not just valuing male comfort more but centering attention on it. Similarly, the advancement of people of color is framed, by some, as a loss for white people, having to make room, compete on equal terms, or just coexist with difference. It's about who matters.

Comfort itself is often invoked as though it were a right of the powerful. In June 2018, *CBS This Morning* tweeted, "Border Patrol has reached out and said they are 'very uncomfortable' with the use of the word cages. They say it's not inaccurate and added that they may be cages but people are not being treated like animals." So a cage should not be called a cage, because the discomfort of people *in* cages is overshadowed by the discomfort of people who put them in cages having cages be called by their true names. Similarly, racists have objected to being called racists of late, and well-housed people have talked about how seeing the homeless upsets them. "White nationalist, white supremacist, Western civilization—how did that language become offensive?" said Republican congressman and white supremacist Steve King. Comfort is often a code word for the right to be unaware, the right to have no twinges of one's conscience, no reminders of suffering, the right to be a "we" whose benefits are not limited by the needs and rights of any "them."

In the name of such comfort, part of the population in the United States and in Europe is moving backward, trying to take up residence in the wreckage of white supremacy and patriarchy, perhaps convinced that there is no shelter that shelters us all, that they need to be in places where whiteness and maleness dominate, that scarcity governs the world and hoarding is a necessary strategy. I said "alarm clocks," and I've been calling this process awakening. Those are value-laden terms, but to become more aware of others unlike you and of the systems that regulate the distribution of power and audibility and credibility and value is to awaken.

The opposite is falling into the nightmare that is also such a powerful force in this time, the nightmare of white supremacy and patriarchy, and the justification of violence to defend them. The permission given by the resurgence of white supremacy and misogyny is to not feel, not value, not extend oneself to solidarity with or even awareness of others, to be unaware, unconcerned, uninformed, unconnected. You can see that this is often experienced as a giddy liberation from the obligation to be "politically correct," that is, to treat others as people having value and rights, including the right to tell their version of the story. I call it a nightmare because it is delusional in its fears and its fantasies of grandeur and its intention of making decades of changes evaporate, of shoving new ideas back into the oblivion from which they emerged and returning to a past that never existed. And because it turns truth from something to be determined by the evidentiary processes of science or investigative journalism or other empirical means into something decided by threat and force. Truth is whatever they want it to be, and as their wants shift, it bloats and billows and fades and flaps in the wind. To make a death threat against a storyteller is to believe that might makes right, and even fact.

Despite the backlashes—or because they are backlashes—I remain hopeful about this project of building new cathedrals for new constituencies. Because it is well under way. Because the real work is not to convert those who hate us but to change the world so that haters don't hold disproportionate power and so that others are not sucked into the nightmare. Because the rising generation is better, overall, and because demographics are creating a United States in which nonwhite people will be the majority in a quarter century, because the pace of backlash-exclusion cannot keep up with the rate of diversification, because our stories are more accurate when it comes to the sources of poverty or the reality of climate change or the equality of women, because our stories invite more people in, because these stories invite us to be more generous, more hopeful, more connected, because so much has changed from the dank world I was born into, in which male superiority and white supremacy were only just beginning to be challenged and new languages about the environment, sexuality, power, connection, and pleasure were just being born.

I.

The Shouters
and the Silenced

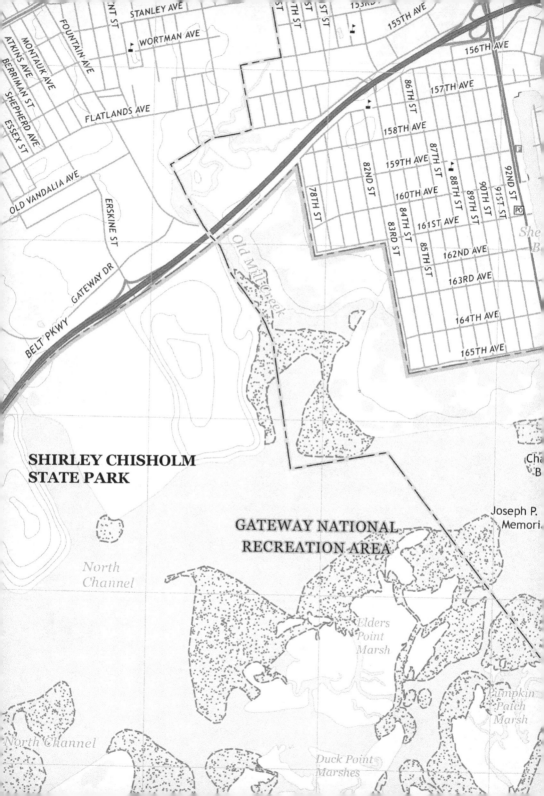

Whose Story (and Country) Is This?

ON THE MYTH OF A "REAL" AMERICA

The common denominator of so many of the strange and troubling cultural narratives coming our way is a set of assumptions about who matters, whose story it is, who deserves the pity and the treats and the presumptions of innocence, the kid gloves and the red carpet, and ultimately the kingdom, the power, and the glory. You already know who. It's white people in general and white men in particular, and especially straight white Protestant men, some of whom are apparently dismayed to find out that there is going to be, as your mom might have put it, sharing. The history of this country has been written as their story, and the news sometimes still tells it this way—one of the battles of our time is about who the story is about, who matters, and who decides.

It is this population we are constantly asked to pay more attention to, and forgive, even when they hate us or seek to harm us. It is toward them we are all supposed to direct our empathy. The exhortations are everywhere. PBS *NewsHour* featured a quiz by Charles Murray in March 2018 that asked, "Do You Live in a Bubble?" The questions assumed that if you didn't know people who drank cheap beer and drove pickup trucks and worked in factories, you lived in an elitist bubble. Among the questions: "Have you ever lived for at least a year in an American community with a population under 50,000 that is not part of a metropolitan area and is not where you went to college? Have you ever walked on a factory floor? Have you ever had a close friend who was an evangelical Christian?"

The quiz was essentially about whether you were in touch with working-class small-town white Christian America, as though everyone who's not Joe the Plumber is Maurice the Elitist. We should know them, the logic goes; they do not need to know us. Less than 20 percent of Americans are white evangelicals, only slightly more than are Latinx, and the former are declining as precipitously as the latter are increasing. Most Americans are urban. The quiz delivered the message, yet again, that the 80 percent of us who live in urban areas are not America; treated non-Protestant and nonwhite people as not America; treated many kinds of underpaid working people (salespeople, service workers, farmworkers) who are not male industrial workers as not America. More Americans work in museums than work in coal, but coalminers are described as sacred beings owed huge subsidies and the sacrifice of the climate, and museum workers—well, no one is talking about their jobs as a totem of our national identity.

PBS added a little note at the end of the bubble quiz: "The introduction has been edited to clarify Charles Murray's expertise, which focuses on white American culture." They didn't mention that he's the author of the notorious book *The Bell Curve*, or explain why someone widely considered racist was welcomed onto the program. Perhaps the actual problem is that white, Christian, suburban, small-town, and rural America includes too many people who want to live in a bubble and think they're entitled to, and that all of us who are not like them are considered menaces and intruders who need to be cleared out of the way.

After all, there was a march in Charlottesville, Virginia, in August 2017, full of white men with tiki torches chanting, "You will not replace us." Which translates as "Get the fuck out of my bubble," a bubble that is a state of mind and a sentimental attachment to a largely fictional former America. It's not everyone in this America; for example, Syed Ahmed Jamal's neighbors in Lawrence, Kansas, rallied to defend him when ICE arrested and tried to deport Jamal, a chemistry teacher and father who had lived in the area for thirty years. It's not all white men; perpetuation of the narrative centered on them is something too many women buy into and some admirable men are trying to break out of.

And the meanest voices aren't necessarily those of actual rural, small-town, or working-class people. In a story about a Pennsylvania coal town named Hazelton, Fox News's wealthy pundit Tucker Carlson recently declared that immigration brings "more change than human beings are designed to digest," the human beings in this scenario being the white Hazeltonians who are not immigrants, with perhaps an intimation that immigrants are not human beings, let alone human beings who have already digested a lot of change. Once again, a small-town white American narrative is being treated as though it's about all of us, or all of us who count, as though the gentrification of immigrant neighborhoods is not also a story that matters, as though Los Angeles County and New York City, both of which have larger populations than most American states, are not America. In New York City, the immigrant population alone exceeds the total population of Kansas (or Nebraska or Idaho or Wyoming and West Virginia, where all those coal miners are). Los Angeles County's population is larger than that of all but nine American states. Thanks to the many problems of our voting system—disenfranchisement, gerrymandering, the electoral college's distortion of the impact of a vote, the distribution of two senators to each state, no matter its size—their voices are magnified already.

In the aftermath of the 2016 election, we were told that we needed to be nicer to the white working class, which reaffirmed the message that whiteness and the working class were the same thing and made the vast nonwhite working class invisible or inconsequential. We were told that Trump voters were the salt of the earth and the authentic sufferers, even though poorer people tended to vote for the other candidate. We were told that we had to be understanding about their choice to vote for a man who threatened to harm almost everyone who was not a straight white cisgender Christian man, because their feelings preempted everyone else's survival. "Some people think that the people who voted for Trump are racists and sexists and homophobes and deplorable folks," Bernie Sanders reprimanded us, though studies and subsequent events showed that many were indeed racists, sexists, and homophobes.

One way we know whose story it is has been demonstrated by who gets excused for hatred and attacks, literal or physical. Early in 2018, the *Atlantic* tried out hiring a writer, Kevin Williamson, who said women who have abortions should be hanged, and then un-hired him under public pressure from people who don't like the idea that a quarter of American women should be executed for exercising jurisdiction over their own bodies. The *New York Times* has hired a few conservatives akin to Williamson, including climate waffler Bret Stephens. Stephens devoted a column to sympathy on Williamson's behalf and indignation that anyone might oppose him.

Sympathy in pro-bubble America often goes reflexively to the white man in the story. The assumption is that the story is about him; he's the protagonist, the person who matters, and when you, say, read Stephens defending Woody Allen and attacking Dylan Farrow for saying her adoptive father, Allen, molested her, you see how much work he's done imagining being Woody Allen, how little being Dylan Farrow or anyone like her. It reminds me of how young women pressing rape charges are often told they're harming the bright future of the rapist in question, rather than that maybe he did it to himself, and that the young woman's bright future should matter, too. The *Onion* nailed it years ago: "College Basketball Star Heroically Overcomes Tragic Rape He Committed."

Who gets to be the subject of the story is an immensely political question, and feminism has given us a host of books that shift the focus from the original protagonist—from Jane Eyre to Mr. Rochester's Caribbean first wife in Jean Rhys's *Wide Sargasso Sea*, from King Lear to Goneril in Jane Smiley's *A Thousand Acres*, from Jason to Medea in Christa Wolf's *Medea*, from Odysseus to Penelope in Margaret Atwood's *The Penelopiad*, and from the hero of the Aeneid to the young woman he marries in Ursula K. LeGuin's *Lucrecia*. There are equivalents in the museum world, such as the diorama depicting the Dutch-Lenape encounter in the American Museum of Natural History in New York, now with texts by an indigenous visual historian, critiquing what's behind the glass. But in the news and political life, we're still struggling over whose story it is, who matters, and at whom our compassion and interest should be directed.

This misdistribution of sympathy is epidemic. The *New York Times* called the man with a domestic-violence history who, in 2015, shot up the Colorado Springs Planned Parenthood, killing three parents of young children, "a gentle loner." And then when the serial bomber who had been terrorizing Austin, Texas, was finally caught in March 2018, too many journalists interviewed his family and friends and let their positive descriptions of the man stand, as though they were more valid than what we already knew: he was an extremist and a terrorist who set out to kill and terrorize Black people in a particularly vicious and cowardly way. He was a "quiet, 'nerdy' young man who came from 'a tight-knit, godly family," the *Times* let us know in a tweet, while the *Washington Post*'s headline noted that he was "frustrated with his life," which is true of millions of young people around the world who don't get a pity party and also don't become terrorists. The *Daily Beast* got it right with a subhead about a recent right-wing terrorist, the one who blew himself up in his home full of bomb-making materials: "Friends and family say Ben Morrow was a Bible-toting lab worker. Investigators say he was a bomb-building white supremacist."

Yet when a teenage boy took a gun to his high school in Maryland and used it to murder Jaelynn Willey in March 2018, the newspapers labeled him "lovesick," as though premeditated murder was just a natural reaction to being rejected by someone you dated. In a powerfully eloquent editorial in the *New York Times*, Marjory Stoneman Douglas student Isabelle Robinson wrote about the excuses peddled for the mass murderer who took seventeen lives at her school on Valentine's Day 2018. She noted a "disturbing number of comments I've read that go something like this: Maybe if Mr. Cruz's classmates and peers had been a little nicer to him, the shooting at Stoneman Douglas would never have occurred." As she observed, this puts the burden—and then the blame—on peers to meet the needs of boys and men who may be hostile or homicidal.

This framework suggests we owe them something, which feeds a sense of entitlement, which sets up the logic of payback for not delivering what they think we owe them. Elliot Rodgers set out to massacre the members of a sorority at UC Santa Barbara in 2014 because he believed that sex with attractive women was a right of his that women were violating, and that another right of his was to punish any or all of them unto death. He killed six people and injured fourteen. Nikolas Cruz, the Marjory Stoneman Douglas murderer, said, "Elliot Rodgers will not be forgotten." The man who killed ten and injured fourteen in Toronto in April 2018 also praised Rodgers in an online post.

Women often internalize this sense of responsibility for men's needs. Stormy Daniels felt so responsible for going to a stranger's hotel room in 2006 that she felt obliged to provide the sex he wanted and she didn't. She told Anderson Cooper, "I had it coming for making a bad decision, for going to someone's room alone, and I just heard the voice in my head, 'Well, you put yourself in a bad situation and bad things happen, so you deserve this.'" (It's worth noting that she classified having sex with Donald Trump as "bad things happen," and the sense in that she deserved it was a punitive one.) His desires must be met. Hers didn't count. Then a tremendous battle happened so that his version of events could stand and hers would not be heard; she was seeking to break the nondisclosure agreement she had signed, a standard piece of legal equipment used against victims of sexual assault to make sure the story the public hears is not hers.

Women are not supposed to want things for themselves, as the *New York Times* reminded us when they castigated Daniels with a headline noting her ambition—a quality that various other high-profile women have also been called out for, but that seems invisible when men have it, as men who act and direct movies and pursue political careers generally do. Daniels had, the *New York Times* told us in a profile of the successful entertainer, "an instinct for self-promotion," and "her competitive streak [was] not well concealed." She intended to "bend the business to her will." The general implication is that any woman who's not a doormat is a dominatrix.

Recently, people have revisited a 2010 political-science study that tested the response to fictitious senatorial candidates, identical except for gender: "regardless of whether male politicians were generally preferred over female politicians, participant voters only reacted negatively to the perceived power aspirations of the female politician." The authors of the study characterized this reaction as "moral outrage." How dare she seek power. How dare she want things for herself rather than for others—even though seeking power may be a means to working on behalf of others. How dare she consider the story to be about her or want to be the one who determines what the story is.

And then there are the #MeToo and #TimesUp movements. We've heard from hundreds, perhaps thousands, of women about assaults, threats, harassment, humiliation, coercion, of campaigns that ended careers, pushed them to the brink of suicide. Many men's response to this is to express sympathy for men. The film director Terry Gilliam was the voice of the old ways when he said, "I feel sorry for someone like Matt Damon, who is a decent human being. He came out and said all men are not rapists, and he got beaten to death. Come on, this is crazy!" Matt Damon has not actually been beaten to death. He is one of the most highly paid actors on earth, which is a significantly different experience than being beaten to death. The actor Chris Evans did much better with this shift in perspective, saying, "The hardest thing to reconcile is that just because you have good intentions doesn't mean it's your time to have a voice."

But the follow-up story to the #MeToo upheaval has too often been: How do the consequences of men hideously mistreating women affect men's comfort? Are men okay with what's happening? There have been too many stories about men feeling less comfortable, too few about how women might be feeling more secure in offices where harassing coworkers may have been removed or are at least a bit less sure about their right to grope and harass. Men are insisting on their comfort as a right. Dr. Larry Nassar, the Michigan State University doctor who molested more than a hundred young gymnasts, objected, on the grounds that it interfered with his comfort, to having to hear his victims give statements during his criminal trial, describing what he did and how it impacted them. These girls and young women had not been silent; they had spoken up over and over, but no one with power—sometimes not even their own parents—would listen and take action, until the *Indianapolis Star* reported, in 2016, on the assaults by Nassar and many other adult men in gymnastics. It was not the women's story until then. It seldom is. Or was.

We are, as a culture, moving on to a future with more people and more voices and more possibilities. Some people are being left behind, not because the future is intolerant of them but because they are intolerant of this future. White male Protestants from the dominant culture are welcome, but, as Chris Evans noted, the story isn't going to be about them all the time, and they won't always be the ones telling it. It's about all of us. White Protestants are already a minority, and nonwhite people will become a voting majority in 2044 or thereabouts.

This country has room for everybody who believes that there's room for everybody. For those who don't—well, that's why there's a battle about whose story it is to tell.

Nobody Knows

When I was eighteen, I spent several months working as a bus girl at a diner. It was a cheerful-looking place, facing San Francisco Bay. The kitchen was L-shaped: the owner stood in the short end of the L with the coffee makers and the cash register, and I was often at the other end, by the dishwashing machine, out of sight. In between were the prep counters and an eight-burner stove, where the cook was stationed. He was a middle-aged drinker with blood-shot eyes, who would unexpectedly grab me from behind. No one seemed to notice, and in that decade before Anita Hill brought "sexual harassment" into the popular lexicon, I couldn't articulate that this was something that violated my rights as well as something that repulsed and rattled me. I couldn't articulate it at all, because in that era we were supposed to take it in stride, learn to cope, not make a big deal out of it, anything but complain and expect intervention.

Around the time I wrote this piece, a customer grabbed a waitress's butt on closed-circuit camera, and the subsequently posted footage let us see her turn around without a moment's hesitation and throw him to the floor; the surrounding story let us know that her manager supported her and so did the police: he was arrested and charged with assault. Her confidence about her rights and the people who backed her up startled me: I had been so used to being on my own in those situations; I had been formed in an era different from hers.

After a few weeks of these unwelcome surprises, I made sure that the next time the cook came for me, I was holding a tray of clean glasses. He grabbed me; I yelped and let go of the tray. The shattering glass made a cacophony. The owner, another middle-aged man, rushed over and chewed out the cook—the glasses were audible and valuable in a way I was not.

Underlings get a reputation for being duplicitous because they sometimes resort to indirect means when straightforward ones are not available. When I was an underling, the only way I knew to make a man stop grabbing me was to trick a more powerful man into laying down the law. I had no authority, or had reason to believe I had none. "When you're a star, they let you do it" has its corollary in "When you're nobody, it's hard to stop them from doing it."

The assumption that I was nobody didn't always fit, even in my youth. A decade after I dropped that tray, I was interviewing a man for my first book. He was married, near my parents' age, but when we were alone for the interview, he got excited and amorous. I could tell that he regarded our interaction as off the record, perhaps because young women were categorically inaudible. I wanted to shout at him, *I am making the public record right now.* Yet had he regarded me with respect, I would have known less about who he was—and thought more of him.

It is an old truism that knowledge is power. The inverse and opposite possibility—that power is often ignorance—is rarely aired. The powerful swathe themselves in obliviousness in order to avoid the pain of others and their own relationship to that pain. It is they from whom much is hidden, and they who are removed from the arenas of the poor and powerless. The more you are, the less you know.

In my neighborhood in San Francisco, for example, white women like me don't need to know that blue is a gang color, but if a young Latino man does not know this, he may be in danger (not least from the police). Similarly, knowing the strategies that women use to be safe around men is, for men, optional, if they ever think about the issue in the first place. (There's a college classroom exercise of asking all students what they do to try to avoid rape, which generally causes women to recite long lists of cautions and avoidances, and men to look blank.) Every subordinate has a strategy for survival, which relies, in part, on secrecy; every unequal system preserves that secrecy and protects the powerful: better the sergeant not know how the privates tolerate him, the master not know that the staff have lives beyond servitude and, perhaps, scorn for whom they serve with apparent deference.

All the world is not a stage: backstage and beyond the theater are important territories, too. There, people at all levels of power act outside the limelight, out of reach of the official rules. For underlings, this can mean a measure of freedom from a system that represses them; for those who wield power, it allows rank hypocrisy. Often they act with the confidence that the people who see them do not matter or cannot affect their reputation among those who do. Because it's not just the knowledge itself that matters, of course— it's also important who knows, whose knowledge it is. You could say that when the powerful insist that nobody knows, what they mean is that their acts are witnessed by nobodies. Nobody knows.

In the mid-seventies, when she was sixteen, my friend Pam Farmer was a page in the US House of Representatives, not long after female pages were first appointed. Over dinner recently, Pam told me that one day, in the Republican cloakroom, she was standing nearby when congressman Sam Steiger from Arizona made a sneeringly sexual remark to sixty-something congresswoman Millicent Fenwick from New Jersey. Another congressman, Barry

Goldwater Jr., happened to be within earshot. He rebuked his colleague: "Would you say this in front of your granddaughter?" Steiger was flustered. He apologized—to Goldwater: it mattered that there was another man with power who had witnessed the event, not that Pam could have been his granddaughter or that Fenwick deserved respect. Neither woman was of consequence. Somebody knew.

A more recent example: last December, female clerks came forth to accuse Alex Kozinski, a judge on the US Court of Appeals for the Ninth Circuit, of forcing them to view pornography with him. These women described how they navigated around the man; they felt obliged to treat him and his despicable behavior as an obstacle that could not be budged, like a mountain range. Alexandra Brodsky, a civil rights attorney, wrote on Twitter, "Glad to see another open secret in print. In law school, everyone knew." But everybody who knew was nobody, at least compared to a federal judge. When an investigative journalist compiled the voices of several of these nobodies into something with clout, the judge resigned as a result.

Perhaps it's not that knowledge is power, but that some knowledge has power and some is stripped of the power it deserves. The powerful lack the knowledge; the knowledge lacks the power. In a just society, if you say, truthfully, that someone assaulted you, that remark should have consequences. An open secret among those without the power to act is knowledge that is, quite literally, inconsequential. On other occasions, knowledge is received, but only reluctantly, as a result of lawsuits and settlement payments. Once the powerful know that the public knows—as when the Murdoch family was faced with exposure of Fox News CEO Roger Ailes's long history of sexual abuse of employees—they finally feel pressure to act.

The allegations about the movie producer Harvey Weinstein paint the picture of a man who went to extraordinary lengths to make somebodies into nobodies. He treated women as people without rights, people who did not have jurisdiction over their own bodies. He threatened to ruin the career of anyone who acted in her own interests instead of his. The revelations of the elaborate machinery designed to turn these women into nobodies were almost as stunning as the accounts of those alleged intimidation campaigns, assaults, and rapes. More than a hundred women, some of them very famous, had been kept silent beyond their personal circles. Millions of dollars had been spent and many people employed in this service, including former Mossad spies and one of the country's most prominent lawyers.

The Weinstein revelations spurred a reexamination of who was audible and who mattered. The persistent harassment in many industries—not just tech and film but also agricultural work, restaurant work, hotel work—was finally acknowledged: abuse, denigration, and assault had long been regarded as officially unacceptable but permissible as long as the public didn't know that those in charge had been aware. When management knew, they generally did nothing until the fact that they had known was exposed. A change in who is audible is a change in who is somebody.

Lots of people knew what nobody knew, for decades, before the isolated dots were connected into a picture that the powerful could no longer look away from. Willed ignorance has been a dam holding back consequences. These torrents of information come about as women's status shifts back and forth between somebody and nobody, as people who'd been silenced are heard.

So often a man who believes that women have no voice is indignant when he discovers that someone is listening to them. It's a struggle to own the narrative. In 2011, when Dominique Strauss-Kahn, then the head of the International Monetary Fund, allegedly—a word I must use because the prosecutor dropped the criminal case, as he often did when it came to powerful men—sexually assaulted a New York City hotel worker named Nafissatou Diallo, his friend Bernard-Henri Lévy defended him. "The Strauss-Kahn I know, who has been my friend for twenty years and who will remain my friend, bears no resemblance to this monster," he wrote in an essay.

Lévy claimed an authority based on the premise that his friend had only one face—the one he showed to powerful men. It was willful inanity, perhaps gleaned from a lifetime of obliviousness about the lives of nobodies; or perhaps it was an insistence that truth, like women, can be bullied into behaving. Soon after, several more women emerged with accusations of sexual assault against Strauss-Kahn, and he settled a civil suit with Diallo. He had been considered a plausible candidate for the presidency of France before these women exposed his other face. For a while it seemed like an African refugee woman was going to be treated as equal to a powerful white man, and then she wasn't.

It's noteworthy how common assaults like Strauss-Kahn's are, so normal that, in 2018, several national hotel chains—after years of pressure from workers—introduced "panic buttons" for cleaning staff. Which is a way of saying that a lot of men who can afford to stay in a good hotel believe that hotel cleaning women cannot afford to speak up, and until now they've been largely right. In the fall of 2018, hotel workers struck at Marriott hotels in many US cities, winning panic buttons, among their concessions. Vox reported, "And for the first time, the company has agreed to ban guests who have a history of sexually harassing workers."

Twenty years ago, I knew that I was moving on from the backstage world. It was as if I had immigrated to another country or been deported from my home. With the transition came an invitation to shift my loyalties and forget where I had long resided. As a writer,

I am someone whose job it is to hear and to tell the stories of the powerless. That means I have power, including power to intervene in the power imbalances that so often manifest as audibility imbalances, and so I am now a person from whom things are hidden by the perpetrators and someone not always assumed to be an ally by the powerless.

I had been the confidante of many young women, and then found that I was too often banished to the company of the powerful and deceived. Some years ago, I spent several days with a group of people. On the last day, one young woman opened up to me about a powerful older man among us who had pressured and harassed her during our time together. He had hidden his pursuit from those in the group he considered to be somebodies, which now included me. I was furious on behalf of his target, and to a lesser extent on behalf of the man's wife, but I was also disgusted to have been so deceived.

I had been ushered into an unwitting audience to a lie. Some of the younger women in our group had known what was going on but had remained silent beyond their circle. I had hitherto been part of that circle. Like the law students and clerks warning one another about Kozinski, we had whispered among ourselves about avoiding certain men and rolled our eyes as another duplicitous performance was staged. Now I was on the outside.

We talk about empathy and compassion as virtues, but they are also active practices of paying attention to other people. In this way, we understand others and the world beyond our own experience. I pay attention to you because you matter, and if you ignore me, it's because I don't. The psychologist Dacher Keltner, who has studied the relationship between empathy and power, has written that "while people usually gain power through traits and actions that advance the interests of others, such as empathy, collaboration, openness, fairness, and sharing; when they start to feel powerful or enjoy a position of privilege, those qualities begin to fade. The powerful are more likely than other people to engage in rude, selfish, and unethical behavior."

Keltner's work demonstrates that the powerful are antisocial or afflicted with "self-focused social-cognitive tendencies" that may "facilitate unethical behavior." In 2011, Keltner and his colleagues analyzed previous studies of upper-class people and found evidence of "unethical decision-making tendencies," lying, cheating, and lower rates of altruism and charitable giving. It also turns out, according to another study, that drivers of luxury cars are more likely to cut off other drivers than wait their turn, and according to yet another, that the powerful are more likely to take candy from children.

Sometimes being immune to the influence of others is a foundation for integrity—Eyal Press has explored this in writing about dissidents who stand apart from their peers during genocides and other crimes. But it can also breed indifference and license cruelty, especially when it's obliviousness to the less powerful. Studies show how much less influenced—that is, how much less aware—the powerful are, how much less their brains engage in mirroring activity. Mirroring is how we replay the actions of others in our minds to connect to what they are doing and feeling. Or we don't, and fail to make a connection; this is a cognitive process as well as an emotional one. It may be instinctive, but it can also be practiced. Or abandoned.

Inequality makes liars of all of us, and only a democracy of power leads to a democracy of information. But underlings know both versions of the two-sided; the powerful seem to know only one, or refuse to know the other. They can conjure an act of erasure: these things have not happened if no one of high status knows.

If power generates a cushion of obliviousness around it, those of us with power need to counter it. That means, first, treating people with respect, regardless of their status: not taking the invitation to disdain or ignore. It means, if you have some power—and most of us have some in some contexts even if we lack it in others—being aware of how your status may cut you off from what others know and may share among themselves; it means knowing that you do not know.

A more radical response is to try to undo the inequality. It means being critical of the forces that create inequality and re-membering that they create asymmetries of audibility and impact. The unexamined life is not worth living, as the aphorism goes, but perhaps an honorable and informed life requires examining others' lives, not just one's own. Perhaps we do not know ourselves unless we know others.

And if we do, we know that nobody is nobody.

They Think They Can Bully the Truth

ON THE LIES OF THE POWERFUL
AND THE POWER OF LIES

Cousin to the noun *dictator* is the verb *dictate*. There are among us people who assume their authority is so great they can dictate what happened; that their assertions will override witnesses, videotapes, evidence, the historical record; that theirs is the only voice that matters, and it matters so much it can stand tall atop the conquered facts. Lies are aggressions. They are attempts to trample down the facts and those who hold them, and they lay the grounds for dictatorships, the little ones in families, the big ones in nations.

Black Lives Matter has focused attention on police officers who continued to insist on their version of events when there was videotaped evidence to the contrary, or when physical evidence and eyewitnesses contradicted their account of events. You realize that they had assumed they could dictate reality, because for decades they actually had, and they were having a hard time adjusting to reality dictating back. As one of the Marx Brothers quipped long ago, "Who you gonna believe, me or your own eyes?" The police assumed it was neither our eyes nor the evidence.

In February 2015, two San Francisco policemen shot a twenty-year-old man, Amilcar Perez-Lopez, to death. All the bullets entered him from behind—four went into his torso through his back—but the policemen claimed they shot the Cho'rti' Mayan immigrant from Guatemala in self-defense because he was rushing them. They did not face consequences—for lying, or for taking the life of a young man trying to get by in a strange land. Two months later, in North Charleston, South Carolina, Walter Scott was shot by a policeman while he, too, fled. He, too, died of bullets to the back, but his killer claimed self-defense in an account that differed dramatically from the videotape (which appears to show the officer planting a weapon on the victim after he had fallen) and eyewitness accounts. Scott's killer got a twenty-year sentence.

That victims will remain voiceless was the presumption behind much of the sexual abuse that's been uncovered in the #MeToo era. Getting away with it is the same thing as assuming that no one will know, because your victim will be intimidated or shamed into silence, or that if he or she speaks up they can be discredited or menaced back into silence, or that even if they don't shut up no one will believe them because your credibility crushes theirs. That yours is the only version that counts, even if you have to use savage means to make it so. Jane Mayer and Ronan Farrow reported, of former New York attorney general Eric Schneiderman's four victims, "All have been reluctant to speak out, fearing reprisal."

Most of us think of truth as something that arises from facts that exist independently of our wills and whims; we have no choice in the matter, but we also believe in some sort of objective reality—either a thing did or did not happen, a sentence was or was not said, a substance is or is not poison. (And, yes, I read lots of postmodern theory once upon a time and know all the counterarguments, but that's not what I'm talking about.) What's clear now is that most is not all, that a minority of us think they can enforce a version of reality divorced from factuality, and that they always have. It corrupts everything around them, and the corruption begins within them.

There are lies subordinates tell to avoid culpability, but they tend to be about specific things (I did not eat the cake, I did not show up late) or survival (I am not undocumented), while these fact-bullies force responses on others, as when a menacing father insists that his whole family pretend that everything is fine and they adore him and last night didn't happen. Gaslighting is a collective cultural phenomenon, too, and it makes cultures feel crazy the way it does individual victims. That we are supposed to pretend that mass shootings and the epidemic gun death rate have nothing to do with the availability of guns is insane.

Of late we have again witnessed the indignation that arises in the powerful when it turns out other people have things to say and that they might be listened to and believed. Congressman Jim Jordan was outraged that nine former wrestlers reported that when Jordan was the assistant wrestling coach at Ohio State, he knew but did nothing about their sexual abuse by the team doctor. A few months into 2019, congressman Devin Nunes followed up a $250 million lawsuit against two parody Twitter accounts ("Devin Nunes's Cow" and "Devin Nunes's Mom") and Republican strategist Liz Mair with a $150 million lawsuit against newspapers for reporting on him. Defenders of Darla Shine, wife of former Fox honcho Bill Shine (briefly also the White House communications director), claimed that she was being smeared by having her own words recirculated (words that, according to the *Washington Post*, "question[ed] why white people would be labeled racist for using the n-word while black people would not, defending the

Confederate battle flag, and highlighting instances of black-on-white crime").

Feminism, like many other human-rights movements, has been a process of amplifying voices until they can hold their own, and of solidarity, so that small voices can be cumulatively loud enough to counter the dictators—what you could call the *Horton Hears a Who* theory of audibility. Thus have so many recent cases—from Bill Cosby to Fox News CEO Roger Ailes to Harvey Weinstein to Brett Kavanaugh—been built by many other women coming forward to support the testimony of the woman or women who broke the ice.

In 2014, singer Kesha sued to be released from her recording contract on the grounds that her producer, Dr. Luke, aka Luke Gottwald, had raped and otherwise abused her and that she had almost no creative control over her own music. (A year earlier, her fans had started a Free Kesha petition.) Gottwald and the corporation refused to release her from the contracts she signed in her mid-teens, so there was a trial that brought more attention to the situation—when she lost, she remained stuck with him, hostage to a man she seems to dread and loathe. Now, four years later, he's suing her because "Gottwald's music career will never recover from the damage she has caused." That is, by her speaking up, with the implication that a superstar singer with a series of #1 hits would remain voiceless. But also, if you assume that Kesha is telling the truth (and I find her credible), Dr. Luke and his backers are blaming her for what he did, or for not keeping it secret. They assume he had a right to impunity, which is a right to do what you like and dictate the reality around it, a right to confront no competing versions, even from the other parties involved.

Meanwhile, the radio host who groped Taylor Swift at a 2013 meet-and-greet and then unsuccessfully sued her for saying so—

since her speaking up resulted in his being fired—complains he's afraid to talk to women (perhaps because talking to a woman and grabbing a woman's ass are apparently so hard for him to tell apart, a kind of confusion we're hearing about from many men who are now "afraid to talk to" women). He says he wants to tell her, "How can you live with yourself? You ruined my life." That seems to be his way of saying that he was shocked to find that one of the most powerful figures in pop music had a voice, and people believed her when she used it. During the trial that may be her greatest performance to date, Swift noted that, contrary to accusations and long-established conventions, she had no responsibility to protect her assailant: "I'm not going to let you or your client make me feel in any way that this is my fault. Here we are years later, and I'm being blamed for the unfortunate events of his life that are the product of his decisions—not mine." She was going after the assumption that no matter what he did, she has to keep life pleasant for him. That no truth contrary to his convenience can be allowed.

Perhaps rather than power, we should talk about *powers*, the ones we can generate ourselves and the ones that people give to us or withhold from us. The power of being believed is distributed as unequally as any out there. The police have assumed that they have more than the people they target; men have assumed they have more than women, whites more than nonwhites. We are in an era of leveling out who has this precious asset. Credibility is not inherent; it resides in how people respond. And those who are silenced beforehand don't even get a chance at credibility.

More and more I come to see the compulsive, frenetic pace of lies by the president as a manic version of that prerogative to dictate reality. It's a way of saying, "I determine what's real and you suck it up, even if you know it's bullshit." When you're a star, they let you do it, and the size of your stardom can be measured in how much you can force people to accept—or pretend to accept—contrary to their own intelligence and orientation and ethics. This is, after all, the liar who, at CIA headquarters on January 21, 2017, told hundreds of CIA employees—skeptics whose profession is the collection and verification of facts—easily disproved lies about the size of his inauguration and the state of the weather the day before. It's unlikely any of them believed him, but perhaps another quality of the powerful is settling for surface appearances, for obliging others to engage in reciprocal lies.

That day, the new president told the CIA, "And the reason you're my first stop is that as you know I have a running war with the media. They are among the most dishonest human beings on earth. Right? And they sort of made it sound like I have this feud with the intelligence community." Which he did, since he'd compared them to Nazi Germany a few weeks before, but he tends to praise to their faces those he attacks behind their backs, as he's done with British prime minister Theresa May (and then denied the earlier statements; the *Washington Post*'s headline read, "Trump denies he said something that he said on a tape that everyone has heard"). One imagines that he has since childhood never been held accountable; it seems more than possible that, after a lifetime of this, he's convinced he actually dictates reality, or that it doesn't exist or only exists at his whim. That is, he's a nihilist and a solipsist (a friend of mine recently compared him to small children who believe that no one can see them when their eyes are closed).

His lying is sometimes regarded as a distraction or an annoyance, but it is a dangerous thing in itself, and he is himself a product of a system of producing and enforcing lies. Trump insisted in his astonishing summer 2018 meeting with Putin in Helsinki that we take Putin's word over that of US intelligence, the world's news agencies, and a lot of senators and congresspeople. The thing to remember here about an assault on truth is that it's an assault.

His followers have had their minds weaponized by decades of Fox News and right-wing pundits promoting conspiracies and denying crucial phenomena, including the important roles immigrants play in our economy and the urgent reality of human-caused climate change. The country is now in a sort of civil war, and part of what is at stake are truth and facts in the form of documented history, scientific fact, political accountability, and adherence to the law, as well as the methodologies by which facts will be determined and the presumption that facts matter.

In "The Prevention of Literature," George Orwell wrote,

> A totalitarian state is in effect a theocracy, and its ruling caste, in order to keep its position, has to be thought of as infallible. But since, in practice, no one is infallible, it is frequently necessary to rearrange past events in order to show that this or that mistake was not made, or that this or that imaginary triumph actually happened. . . . Totalitarianism demands, in fact, the continuous alteration of the past, and in the long run probably demands a disbelief in the very existence of objective truth.

The internet has produced its own form of informational relativism. Facebook took heat for its protracted refusal, amid what was supposed to be an informational cleanup, to ban InfoWars—which, among the other conspiracy theories it's pushed, claimed the Sandy Hook massacre of children was a hoax and the teenage Parkland mass shooting survivors were "crisis actors." Asked about the continued presence of InfoWars, Facebook News Feed head John Hegeman said, "I think part of the fundamental thing here is that we created Facebook to be a place where different people can have a voice. And different publishers have very different points of view." That some of them are libelous and destructively false doesn't seem to faze him (Sandy Hook parents, six of whom sued InfoWars, have received threats from people directed by InfoWars to believe that the massacre was "a hoax to take away your guns"). This is a consequence of Internet companies' claiming to be neutral platforms rather than information organizations, with the responsibilities that have always come with that role. This is the result of their desire to serve any product to any customer, as long as it's profitable.

Facebook did finally ban InfoWars in August 2018, and then, in February 2019, removed twenty-two more Facebook pages tied to Jones, shortly after CEO Mark Zuckerberg told tech journalist Kara Swisher, "But at the end of the day, I don't believe that our platform should take that down because I think there are things that different people get wrong—I don't think that they're intentionally getting it wrong. It's hard to impugn intent and to understand the intent. I just think as important as some of those examples are, I think the reality is also that I get things wrong when I speak publicly." Which is hard to read as anything but a libertarian "everyone's entitled to their own facts" posture that ignores the unequal impact of, say, conspiracy theories and death threats on social media. "From their mountaintop they see the playing field is level" is one of my old adages.

Meanwhile, Safiya Umoja Noble's book *Algorithms of Oppression: How Search Engines Reinforce Racism* proposes that one driving force behind Charleston church mass murderer Dylann Roof's racism was Google. In a piece on Noble's book, *Pacific Standard*'s James McWilliams reports that Roof did a search for "black on white crime" and was directed to a website of the Council of Conservative Citizens, a white supremacist organization that promulgates lies. Google owns YouTube, which, the *Wall Street Journal* reported in February 2018, offers recommendations to viewers that "often present divisive, misleading or false content." Tech critic Zeynep Tufekci noted that YouTube's "algorithm seems to have concluded that people are drawn to content that is more extreme than what they started with—or to incendiary content in general," and it gives them what they want or think they want, whether or not it's good for them or us or the record. The most powerful corporations on earth have, in other words, concluded that lies are profitable and pursued that profit.

As Hannah Arendt famously said, "The ideal subject of totalitarian rule is not the convinced Nazi or the convinced Communist, but people for whom the distinction between fact and fiction (i.e., the reality of experience) and the distinction between true and false (i.e., the standards of thought) no longer exist." Making those distinctions, doing the work to be clear, is resistance. It consists in part of supporting and reading good news outlets (including the newspapers whose financial basis has been undermined by the internet), and being informed about both the news they report and the historical background to the current crises to be found in books (and in universities, which makes it worth noting that the value of a humanities education is also under attack; one of its values is making people thoughtful sifters of data, who are well-grounded in history). It consists of maintaining your capacity to fact-check and sift and evaluate information and your independence of mind. Solidity and steadfastness are key to resistance, and to clarity about who you are and what you believe. Principles are contagious, and though we need direct and dramatic action, the catalytic power of myriad people standing on principle and living by facts matters, too. It means holding yourself and those around you to high standards not only of truth but of accuracy.

Equality is also a weapon against lies. If the privilege of dictating leads to dictatorship, then the obligation to be accountable leads to its opposite. Producing that accountability even on a small scale—with police watchdog groups, with support for this victim of sexual assault or that target of racism, with fact-checking and a commitment to accuracy even in your personal conversations—is resistance that matters. The job before us now is to produce it on a national and international scale, with a force that cannot be overcome by lies.

Unconscious Bias
Is Running for President

Unconscious bias is running for president again. Unconscious bias has always been in the race, and unconscious bias's buddy, Institutional Discrimination, has always helped him along, and as a result all of our presidents have been men, and all but one white, and that was not even questionable until lately. This makes who "seems presidential" a tautological ouroboros chomping hard on its own tail. The Republican Party has more than embraced its status as the fraternity of conscious bias, binge-drinking resentment until it passes out and becomes unconscious bias. But this also affects the Democratic Party and its voters, where maybe bias should not be so welcome.

One of the curious, ugly facts about the 2020 election is that white men are a small minority of people who vote Democratic, but they have wildly disproportionate control of the money and media and look to have undue influence over the current race for the nomination. This is just one of the many ways that "one person one vote" isn't really what we have, because we have all this other stuff that decides who gets to vote (aka voter suppression) and whom we get to vote for. In 2016 white men were approximately

34 percent of the electorate but not quite 11 percent of the votes for the Democratic candidate, because more than two thirds of them voted for Trump or third-party candidates. Black voters were also about 11 percent of the Democratic vote total (and Black women voted 94 percent Democratic, the highest total of any major social group). Black and Latina women alone constitute a proportion of the Democratic electorate comparable to white men. So, in a completely egalitarian system, what Black voters or nonwhite women want in a Democratic candidate should matter at least as much as what white men want.

But power is not distributed equally, and too many white men—politicians, media powerhouses, funders, people I crash into on social media—are using theirs in familiar ways. Also, a hell of a lot of them are medaling in unconscious bias. In 2016 I wrote, "With their deep belief in their own special monopoly on objectivity, slightly too many men assure me that there is no misogyny in their subjective assessments or even no subjectivity and no emotion driving them, and there are no grounds for other opinions since theirs is not an opinion." I wish that weren't still the case, and I fear how it will yet again affect election outcomes.

I've just spent a month watching white male people in particular arguing about who has charisma or relatability or electability. They speak if these were objective qualities, and as if their own particular take on them were truth or fact rather than taste, and as if what white men like is what everyone likes, or as if white men are who matters, which is maybe a hangover from the long ugly era when only white men voted. It's a form of self-confidence that verges on lunacy, because one of the definitions of that condition is the inability to distinguish between subjective feelings and objective realities.

Ryan Lizza, fired from the *New Yorker* for undisclosed sexual misconduct, tweeted, "The Kamala Harris fundraising numbers drive home just how impressive Pete Buttigieg's fundraising numbers are," when hers were nearly twice as large, and maybe who has money to donate and why white men have always been carried forward and Black women have always been held back are relevant things here. One notable thing about the 2016 election is that some of the leading pundits whose misogyny helped shape the race—including Matt Lauer, Charlie Rose, Mark Halperin, Glenn Thrush—were later charged with sexual abuse or harassment; that is, their public bias was paralleled by appalling private misconduct. Fox's Bill O'Reilly and Roger Ailes were outed earlier; heads of networks, directors, and producers have also been outed as serial sexual abusers in charge of our dominant narratives.

Meanwhile, the *New York Times*, in all its august unbearability, published this prize sentence in a piece about Joe Biden's failure to offer Anita Hill an apology she found adequate: "Many former Judiciary Committee aides and other people who participated did not want to talk on the record because they feared that scrutiny of Mr. Biden's past conduct would undermine the campaign of the candidate some think could be best positioned to defeat President Trump, whose treatment of women is a huge issue for Democrats." I think that translates as, "Let's run a guy whose treatment of women is an issue, and let's ignore that treatment because, even so, we think that he's best positioned to defeat the guy whose treatment of women is an issue. Also, fuck treatment of women, especially this Black woman, as an issue, really."

Sometimes these white guys with outsized platforms say shit like James Comey did when he complained that his erstwhile classmate Amy Klobuchar was "annoyingly smart," perhaps because women are not supposed to be like that, in his worldview. Another man had the temerity to explain to me that "the really smart wonks don't end up being the media stars needed to win the presidency, i.e., Hillary Clinton—super smart, knows the facts, but comes off as smug and all-knowing. I get this from Kamala Harris too." In other words, he assumes that they are women who know too much and the character defect is theirs, not his. The framework that intelligence is an asset in a man and a defect in a woman is nastily familiar.

A friend of mine posted some praise of Elizabeth Warren, and a man jumped in to say, "It's a moot point because she's not going to get into office. With any luck Bernie Sanders is going to do that." I've heard a lot of white men explain that Warren can't win because she's wonky, and then when I mention that our last two Democratic presidents were famously wonky, I get to hear why they had charisma and Warren doesn't. I am a middle-aged woman and quite possibly wonky myself, or at least stuffed with a lot of obscure information and vocabulary words, so I find Elizabeth Warren kind of magnificent, and if that word "relatable" is not going to die an overdue death, that, too. When she talks about dismantling big tech or calls for impeachment with a voice full of conviction or delivers another of her well-crafted plans to change the world, that's compelling and exactly what I hope to see in a leader. To me, Kamala Harris questioning Jeff Sessions and Brett Kavanaugh until they tremble is riveting and supremely skilled and powerful, which is maybe what we mean by charismatic.

But I'm a woman, so I've always been aware that what I like is not what everyone likes. After all, another friend reported a man saying Warren's voice "makes my balls shrivel," electability apparently tied to the gender-specific sparking of joy in the scrotum. It reminds me of Kanye West saying, of his MAGA hat, "But this hat, it gives me power in a way. My dad and my mom separated, so I didn't have a lot of male energy in my home. There was something about putting this hat on that made me feel like Superman."

West is not white, but he does ace unconscious bias with his widely shared male idea that a president or a presidential candidate should have the same general effect as Viagra, and he does remind me that the 2016 election sometimes seemed to be an erectile referendum.

The problem, as feminist philosopher Kate Manne put it recently, is that what we say now is not just commentary about what is possible: it is shaping what is possible. She said, "If we knew for sure that a candidate couldn't beat Trump, that would be reason not to support them. But electability isn't a static social fact; it's a social fact we're constructing. Part of what will make someone unelectable is people [giving] up on them in a way that would be premature, rather than going to the mat for them." Meanwhile, lots of media outlets have worked hard at associating the women candidates with negative language. "How does Elizabeth Warren avoid a Clinton redux—written off as too unlikeable before her campaign gets off the ground," tweeted Politico. "I Can't Believe Elizabeth Warren Is Losing to These Guys" is the headline of a *Jacobin* article that ties her to the failure.

What makes a candidate electable is in part how much positive coverage they get, and how much positive coverage they get is tied to how the media powers decide who is electable, and so goes the feedback loop. Perry Bacon Jr. at FiveThirtyEight writes, "Because the U.S. is majority white, and because a significant number of Americans have some negative views about nonwhite people and women, a heavy emphasis on electability can be tantamount to encouraging any candidates who aren't Christian white men either not to run in the first place—or to run only if they are willing to either ignore or downplay issues that involve their personal identities." But if a party is majority women and people of color, should the same factors prevail? Shouldn't we have a situation in which white men don't really matter so much?

Unconscious bias is running for president. Anyone advocating for a candidate who's not white or male has to compete not just against the official rivals but against the burden of inequality and prejudice on a playing field approximately as level as the Grand Tetons. It is far from impossible to overcome, but it is extra work that needs to be done. Because equal work for equal pay isn't a thing yet, as long as not being white or male or straight requires all this extra labor and comes with all these extra obstacles.

Voter Suppression Begins at Home

Progressive organizer Annabel Park told the story that made me start to wonder. "I can't stop thinking about this woman I met while door-knocking for Beto in Dallas," Annabel wrote on social media a few days before the 2018 midterm elections, in which Beto O'Rourke was challenging Texas Republican senator Ted Cruz. "She lived in a sprawling low-income apartment complex. After I knocked a couple of times, she answered the door with her husband just behind her. She looked petrified and her husband looked menacing behind her. When I made my pitch about Senate candidate Beto O'Rourke, her husband yelled, 'We're not interested.' She looked at me and silently mouthed, 'I support Beto.' Before I could respond, she quickly closed the door."

Annabel told me afterward, "It's been on my mind. Did she get beaten? That was my fear."

There's a form of voter intimidation that is both widespread and unacknowledged. It's the husbands who bully and silence and control their wives, as witnessed by the dozens of door-to-door canvassers across the country from whom I heard. Wives asked their husbands directly whom the two were going to vote for. Many seemed cowed. Husbands answered the door and refused to let the wife speak to canvassers, or talked or shouted over her, or insisted that she was going to vote Republican even though she was a registered Democrat, or insisted there were no Democrats in the house because she had never told him she was one. A friend in Iowa told me, "I asked the woman who answered the door if she had a plan for voting, and a man appeared, behind her, and said, quite brusquely, 'I'm a Republican.' Before I could reply, he shut the door in my face."

Another friend reported, "A woman I texted in Michigan told me, 'I am not allowed' to vote for the candidate." Many canvassers told me those experiences were common. I did not find stories of the reverse phenomenon—wives dominating their husbands, or husbands pushing their wives to vote for the Democratic candidate. Of course, I talked to people canvassing for Democrats, and domestic violence takes place across the political spectrum, but the bullying they reported seemed to be mostly either to oblige the wife to lean to the right or not to participate at all (and though bullying from the left also exists, it has not been reported to me as a domestic issue).

"The wife spotted me and jumped up from her table to intercept me at the door before I could knock," one canvasser from California told me. "Without saying any words, the wife softly put both hands out in front of her body, palms facing me. She moved her hands from side to side as though to tell me, 'No thank you, please go away without making a noise.'" She was one of many who appeared to be afraid of their husbands.

Going door to door, as I have several times in Northern Nevada since 2004, is an extraordinary experience. You see demographics break down into actual faces, stories, shabby or manicured front yards, see subdivisions and slums, see people who are clear and fierce or indifferent or confused about the upcoming election. You meet people where they live, and some live in captivity, in fear, in subjugation. The violence in domestic violence is best understood as a subset of what is now often called coercive control, an attempt to dominate someone by means that are psychological—and may also be financial, physical, social, political—by preventing them from participating in the larger world and holding opinions of their own and exercising agency over their own bodies, lives, finances, truths. It makes perfect sense that this would apply to voting rights, since it can apply to anything and everything.

The one article on the subject I was able to find, by Danielle Root, noted,

> One of the most common tactics domestic abusers use against survivors is isolating them from family, friends, and community members. . . . Additionally, abusers will often restrict or monitor a survivor's access to the outside world via the telephone or internet. . . . Isolation is particularly problematic for individuals experiencing intimate partner violence who want to vote.

She added, "Election canvassing also presents a unique potential threat to those experiencing intimate partner violence."

My friend Melody had a Nevada man, who never turned off his leaf-blower, roar at her over the din, "This is a RED house! This house is Republican!" Melody told me:

> I say I've come by to speak to Donna. "No, she doesn't want to speak to you." I consider saying, "Looks like this house is kind of purple, since Donna is a Democrat." But then I think, "Maybe he doesn't know. Maybe she just goes into that booth and votes the way she wants without telling him." But what if she doesn't go into a booth? What if they vote at the kitchen table? Does he supervise her ballot? Is she afraid to fill it out according to her own wishes rather than his?

Emily Van Duyn reported in the *Washington Post* on secret groups of Democratic women in Texas, writing,

> Many remain hidden because they want to avoid social conflict and are even fearful of being openly progressive in their community. Their experience of fear and intimidation challenges assumptions about democracy in the United States. That is, in a truly liberal democracy, people should be able to voice their views without fear of retaliation. These women's choice to engage and persist underground also challenges us to reconsider the privilege of being publicly political and the possibility that the things we see on the surface in our communities, the yard signs, the bumper stickers, are not the whole story.

No one knows to what extent this domination reported by canvassers may prevent women from voting according to their own beliefs and agendas, or from participating at all, or whether it's on a scale to affect election outcomes. Of course, there are plenty of right-wing women enthusiastically voting for the conservative of their choice, but when you look at the enormous gender gaps between Democrats and Republicans or hear the myriad door-to-door stories, you recognize that there are many marriages between Democratic women and Republican men, and many Republican men who intend to control their wives' political expression. There have been other kinds of harassment in public and on social media, from the left and center as well as the right, but this intimate oppression seems to be, from the stories I gathered and experienced canvassers I talked to, mostly a conservative phenomenon, and since conservatives are mostly white, probably mostly a white one as well (though coercive control exists among all races and political orientations).

The problem matters for voting rights, whether or not it influences outcomes, and it's also a reminder that many women are not free and equal in their domestic lives. Yet another canvasser reported that one of those husbands, this time in Turlock, California, said, of his wife: "And if she needs to know how to vote, I'll just take her in the back and beat her." He was sort of joking but sort of not. One woman told me, "I had several Republican women contact me privately and ask if their husbands would be able to find out how they voted." Another told me about a husband who confiscated the children's car seats so that his wife could not leave the house with the children to drive to a voting place.

This ordinary, ugly scenario raises another question, about whether the increasingly common practice of filling out mail-in ballots at home takes away the privacy of the voting booth and the ability of women and other family members to act on their beliefs without consequences. It's a reminder of why women's long quest for the vote in the US and elsewhere was such a radical thing. Insisting women should vote was insisting that we should be equal and independent participants in public life, with the right to act on our own behalf and in our own interests. And before widespread voting by mail, voting was literally an act one took in public among other members of the public, a rite of citizenship that seems to be fading, as is so much else of public life.

The women's suffrage movement clashed with laws that defined women as, essentially, the property or wards of their husbands, who had the right to control their bodies, their labor, their earnings, and their assets. It clashed with custom, which held that women's sphere was private life and women's role was deference and obedience to the man of the house. "He's the decision maker" is a phrase I grew familiar with in the stories from canvassers.

The conservative agenda is, of course, what you could call marriage inequality, an asymmetrical relationship in which men hold most of the power. The right to vote according to your own conscience and agenda is really not so different from the right to control your own body or to have equal access and rights in the workplace. It's a right we're meant to have because the laws say we're all equal. But we're not. As with the myriad Republican measures to prevent citizens from voting on the large scale—Crosscheck, voter ID laws, limits on polling places and voting hours—this domestic tyranny is an attempt to limit who decides what this country should be.

Lies Become Laws

Anti-abortion laws are built on anti-abortion lies. Lies about things like who has abortions and why, how abortions work, how women's bodies work, and how fetuses develop. The lies pave the way for the laws.

There are the old lies, like the ones suggesting that the women having abortions are careless child-loathing hussies (51 percent of abortions are among women who were using contraception in the month they became pregnant; 59 percent are among women who are already mothers; 75 percent are among poor and low-income women; 100 percent of unwanted pregnancies involve men). Lately, there's a huge new lie making the rounds—that women and doctors are conspiring to kill babies at birth and calling it abortion. This is a lie that encourages conservatives to regard pregnant women and medical caregivers as ruthless killers who should be hemmed in with yet more laws targeting them. While a lot of older abortion lies were distortions and exaggerations, this one is a complete and dangerous fabrication.

At a late April 2019 rally in Wisconsin, Donald Trump said: "The baby is born. The mother meets with the doctor. They take care of the baby. They wrap the baby beautifully, and then the doctor and the mother determine whether or not they will execute the baby." (The closest thing to this far-fetched scenario is when babies are born with what are sometimes called "conditions incompatible with life" and, at the discretion of the parents, receive palliative care rather than the often tortuous interventions that will postpone but not prevent their deaths.) Fox host Ainsley Earhardt amplified the lie, saying: "I think it backfired on those Democrats when they all said you can have an abortion even after the baby is born or kill the baby after the baby is born." This framework helps portray abortion at any stage, for any reason, as murder.

Crucially, this new lie may have contributed to a climate in which lawmakers in Georgia and Alabama were willing to criminalize medical caregivers and make them subject to new kinds of scrutiny. Under a new Alabama law, as CNN put it: "Any physician who is convicted of performing an abortion in the state would be a Class A felon—the highest level in Alabama." The idea that abortion is murder has been used to justify actual murder: the tenth anniversary of the murder of abortion provider Dr. George Tiller in Wichita, Kansas, was on May 31, 2019; in late 2015 a white gunman with a history of domestic violence shot up a Colorado Planned Parenthood, killing three parents of young children and injuring several others. He called himself "a warrior for the babies." Planned Parenthood provides abortions as a small proportion of its services and—as the nation's frontline supplier of reproductive healthcare, including contraception and sex education—prevents them.

Around the time that this myth of infanticide was being promoted, House whip Steve Scalise, a Republican from Louisiana, had a "born alive discharge petition tracker" on the top of his official government webpage. It is part of a campaign suggesting that abortions regularly result in live births of viable fetuses that are then killed or allowed to die. The huge majority of abortions take place before the embryo or fetus is viable outside the womb; fetuses emerging from abortion procedures alive are extremely rare, but there are federal and state laws regulating these cases, often framed in ways that make them sound both more common and the consequences more homicidal.

There's another lie built into a lot of the new bills: the idea that they prevent the abortion of fetuses with heartbeats. In actual fact, so-called "fetal heartbeat bills" would also apply to embryos that haven't yet become fetuses and whose cells haven't yet become complex organs, including a fully formed heart.* At six weeks the embryo is less than half an inch long. According to obstetrician-gynecologist Dr. Colleen McNicholas, "To say that a six-week pregnancy has a fetal anything is incorrect." She explained to a Huffington Post journalist, "At that point, it really is just these two tubes with a couple of layers of cardiac or heart cells that can vibrate or cause some sort of movement that we use colloquially to talk about a 'fetal heartbeat.'" These bills seem designed to influence public imagination, not accurately register development in utero. Despite that, the Georgia law is supposed to "provide for advising women seeking an abortion of the presence of a detectable human heartbeat."

Some fear the new laws may lead to more widespread criminalization of miscarriages. There are about a thousand cases to date of women whose miscarriages have been criminalized; Jezebel reported recently: "Black women and low-income women are more likely to be arrested for these pregnancy-related charges." Up to 20 percent of known pregnancies, perhaps half of all pregnancies, according

---

*This essay originally appeared in the *Guardian*, which announced shortly afterward that the *Guardian* will no longer use the term "heartbeat bill" in reference to the restrictive abortion bans that are moving through state legislatures in the US. "We want to avoid medically inaccurate, misleading language when covering women's reproductive rights," the *Guardian*'s US editor in chief, John Mulholland, said. "These are arbitrary bans that don't reflect fetal development—and the language around them is often motivated by politics, not science."

to a 2018 study, result in miscarriage. Criminalizing miscarriages means that those capable of being impregnated would, if they had sex with men, run the risk of being punished for common biological events beyond their control. In that world, it's conceivable that if the authorities know you're pregnant, thanks to medical visits (or fertility apps), you risk being charged with the "crime" of having a miscarriage or an abortion, which would be an incentive to avoid healthcare services. In June 2019, an Alabama woman who was shot in the stomach in late 2018 was arrested for manslaughter because her five-month-old fetus died. The woman who shot her was not charged; the argument was that it was fault of the (poor, Black) pregnant woman for getting into a fight. Charges were later dropped.

Like many other states' new laws, the Georgia law bans abortion at a stage of pregnancy so early many women don't know they're pregnant, and if they do find out, they will have to move fast to make the deadlines, and of course the shuttering of clinics, the obstructions such as waiting periods, and other measures create delays. So abortions will remain available, but under increasingly impossible terms because of abortion laws driven by stories about things that don't actually happen.

Some abortions are to complete the process of a miscarriage to protect the mother's life; the 2018 Irish abortion referendum overturning the ban on the procedure was prompted in part by the death of a woman, Dr. Savita Halappanavar, who was having a miscarriage. She was denied a medically necessary abortion as long as there was a fetal heartbeat, even though the fetus would die anyway, and she developed a fatal infection as a result. She wanted the child; she wanted to live; she died a cruel and unnecessary death. Ireland voted in a landslide to overturn the ban.

Meanwhile, Texas is in the process of passing a law that will make women into living coffins, forced to carry dying or doomed fetuses to term. The *Texas Tribune* reports: "The Texas Senate passed a bill on Tuesday that would ban abortions on the basis of the sex, race or disability of a fetus, and criminalize doctors who perform what opponents call 'discriminatory abortions.' Current state law prohibits abortions after 20 weeks of pregnancy, but there are certain exceptions, such as when the pregnancy is not viable or the fetus has 'severe and irreversible' abnormalities. Senate Bill 1033 would do away with those exceptions."

It seems unlikely anyone is seeking an abortion because of the race of the baby, but it does tie into the myth that abortion is part of a eugenics campaign, and US Supreme Court justice Clarence Thomas recently made that charge. The *Washington Post* cited "seven scholars of the eugenics movement; all of them said that Thomas's use of this history was deeply flawed." Sex-selective abortions are so common in Asia that China and India both have a skewed gender balance among the young; but there is no evidence that they represent a significant percentage of abortions in the US.

Sometimes the mostly white, mostly male legislators pushing these lies seem like amoral strategists. Sometimes they just seem like idiots. NBC reports: "The new bill currently introduced by Republicans in the Ohio state house would preclude doctors from pursuing the standard of care in cases of life-threatening ectopic pregnancies"—when a fertilized egg implants outside of the uterus—"and ban private insurance companies from covering it by calling it an abortion and forcing them, instead, to cover a re-implantation procedure whether the woman wanted that or not." Except you can't save an ectopic pregnancy, but by delaying abortion you gamble with the chance that the mother will die. So this is a bill to force a procedure that doesn't exist to save an embryo or fetus who's doomed while risking the life of the mother, who can be saved. It isn't pro-life, it is pro-lie.

Sometimes the bills themselves are flat-out lies: in March 2019 the North Dakota governor signed into law legislation that requires doctors to tell patients that drug-induced abortions are reversible; on June 25, 2019, the American Medical Association filed a lawsuit against the state because the law requires medical providers to make "a patently false and unproven claim unsupported by scientific evidence." The suit also covers another North Dakota law that the AMA says "forces physicians to tell patients that abortion terminates 'the life of a whole, separate, unique, living human being'—a controversial, ideological, and non-medical message—and unconstitutionally forces physicians to act as the mouthpiece of the state."

Michelle Alexander made a really important point in the *New York Times* recently: all that palaver about exemptions for rape just means that rape victims who want abortions will have to try to prove they were raped. Given how rarely men are convicted of rape, and how slow and intrusive and hostile to victims the legal process is, one can imagine the fetus reaching preschool age or maybe kindergarten or possibly law school before the court case is concluded. The *Houston Chronicle* recently reported on a Baptist pastor arrested for raping a teenage relative over and over during a two-year period. The child was thirteen when the assaults began. The newspaper reported that the arrest happened shortly after the pastor testified in favor of "failed House Bill 896 that would have abolished abortions in Texas and opened up the possibility that prosecutors could charge a woman who undergoes the procedure with criminal homicide. The offense can be punishable by the death penalty under current Texas law."

It is another way to intrude into women's lives and terminate their rights. It puts women's lives in the hands of law enforcement and entangles medical decisions with bureaucracies and regulations. And under the Alabama law, there is no incest and rape exemption: the eleven-year-old raped by her father will be sentenced to nine months of pregnancy with all the health risks that entails, as well as the horror. Alabama is one of two states that doesn't terminate the parental rights of rapists, so a victim can be tied to her rapist for life if she doesn't terminate the pregnancy. (Half of states require a rape conviction to terminate paternal rights, and given that only about 2 or 3 percent of rapes result in convictions, they do only slightly more than nothing for rape victims.) The Baptist pastor arrested in Texas had allegedly committed his crimes against the child several years earlier. The law came late to her defense.

Reproductive rights activists have been noting for decades that it would be easier to believe that anti-choice politicians cared about babies if they supported prenatal health, maternal healthcare, early childhood development and education and other resources that support the wellbeing of mothers and children. But you can go further than that. Two scholars published an analysis in the *Journal of the American Medical Association* in 2001 demonstrating that "homicide was in fact the leading cause of mortality during pregnancy and the first postpartum year, accounting for one out of five deaths. Simultaneously, a study in the *Journal of Midwifery & Women's Health* found that an astounding 43% of maternal deaths over eight years in Washington DC, were homicides."

One key way to address this would be gun control, but of course anti-abortion and anti-gun control legislation are often brought to us by the same people, and together the two positions seem to be about unlimited, unfettered power for men, who own and use guns (and kill people) at much higher rates than women. Pew reported that, in 2017, "white men are especially likely to be gun owners: about half (48%) say they own a gun, compared with about a quarter of white women and nonwhite men (24% each) and 16% of nonwhite women."

Anti-abortion advocates have often suggested that an unwanted, unplanned pregnancy is somehow a thing malicious women do on their own. There are intentional, wanted pregnancies achieved through sperm donors and in-vitro fertilization, but pretty much every other pregnancy is a result of a person injecting sperm into a person with eggs through penetrative vaginal sex. There may be cases where the carelessness is hers, there are cases where it's his, there are cases where careful precautions fail, or where wanted pregnancies go terribly wrong.

What we don't talk about often enough is how blurry the boundaries are, how often women are cajoled and pressured and lied to in order to allow, for the sake of penile pleasure, unprotected penetrative sex that can result in pregnancy. The last time I heard a story about a man who violated the agreement to use a condom was last week.** The idea of holding men responsible for unwanted pregnancy is beginning to take hold in some quarters. Imagine if those who impregnate were held as responsible as those who are impregnated. It's a slippery slope, since the decision to terminate should belong to the pregnant person, and of course the goal should not be to criminalize anyone. But recognizing that no one gets pregnant alone and that many pregnancies are as much the responsibility of the person with sperm as the person with an egg is a perspective gaining momentum, and it changes the story,

---

**Among the 2010 sexual assault charges against Julian Assange was violating the agreement to use a condom with both of the women in question. Feminist legal scholar Alexandra Brodsky wrote, in 2017, "Nonconsensual condom removal during sexual intercourse exposes victims to physical risks of pregnancy and disease and, interviews make clear, is experienced by many as a grave violation of dignity and autonomy. Such condom removal, popularly known as "stealthing," can be understood to transform consensual sex into nonconsensual sex." A 2019 report from Australia concluded that one out of three women and one out of five men having sex with men have been victims of nonconsensual condom removal. And, the report notes, "It found women who experience violence from an intimate partner are twice as likely to have their male partner refuse contraception, twice as likely to have an unplanned pregnancy, three times as likely to give birth as a teen and significantly more likely to have five or more births."

or rather undermines the misogynist stories that buttress the anti-abortion position.

An extraordinary story hit the news not long ago. "A police report says a south Mississippi lawmaker punched his wife in the face
after she didn't undress quickly enough when the lawmaker wanted to have sex." Republican representative Doug McLeod allegedly
bloodied his wife's nose; she bled all over the bed and floor and fled
the room, and the police were called. (He has said reports mischarac-
terize what happened.) It's hard to regard the kind of sex he intended
to have as consensual, if a frightened wife was punished for not obey-
ing orders with enough alacrity. It's a little window into the kind of
marriage in which women have little bodily self-determination, in
which their decision to use birth control or refrain from sex during
their most fertile time may be overridden. I looked up McLeod; sure
enough he had introduced a "fetal heartbeat" anti-abortion bill earlier this year.

Reproductive rights are what make women in their fertile years
able to participate fully in public and economic life, to have the
same bodily sovereignty men take for granted, to be free and equal.
I believe the hatred of abortion is often because it gives women an
autonomy and freedom equivalent to that of men, and that hatred
is often expressed by people who show no interest in the health of
infants or wellbeing of children. Or women. And at this point, in
science, facts, and truth. Their lies pave the way for their laws.

The Fall of Men Has Been Greatly Exaggerated

ON KAVANAUGH, GHOMESHI,
AND WHO GETS TO TELL THE STORY

A type specimen is, in biology, the first officially named version of an animal or plant, which comes to represent the characteristics of the species in the popular imagination. I have found, over the years, that humans also utter type specimens—reactive statements that embody a worldview or a fallacy, or the way the former is stuck full of the latter like a porcupine with quills. Their value is in demonstrating clearly and dramatically how some minds work, or how some beliefs act on us, or why shit is fucked up and crazy.

On September 13, 2018, a man uttered so perfect a type specimen of misogyny in all its loopily malicious self-delusion that I made a screenshot of it, as if to enter it into the biological record. This was a good move because the misogynist in question, after fervently defending his tweet, eventually deleted it at some point the next day.

It was about the then anonymous woman who, in a letter to a Democratic senator and congresswoman, said that she had been assaulted by Supreme Court nominee Brett Kavanaugh, but successfully fought him off, when they were both high-school students. The man who tweeted was an Ivy League lawyer named Ed Whelan, and he tweeted at 8:46 p.m. on the West Coast, close to midnight in the nation's capital—if he was indeed in the town where he works as the head of the right-wing Ethics and Public Policy Center—which is late to be tweeting about politics, and one could speculate on what was going on in his head, but he gives speculation a bad name, or maybe a black eye, with his tweet. He tweeted this widening gyre of fantasy about his colleague Brett Kavanaugh's then anonymous accuser:

> Wonder if accuser will say she was sober at time of alleged incident at drinking party. If drunk, how drunk? Cognitive dysfunction, impaired memory, mistaken identity, all compounded by 35 years? (I am of course not saying her drunkenness would excuse anyone else's conduct.)

It is magnificent in its march, addressing in the first sentence not what she said but what she might say if challenged, which is itself a way to challenge her. She will say it; should we believe her? Perhaps this lawyer pictures himself cross-examining her and destroying her in front of a jury.

By the second sentence he's shifted the focus from whether she'd say she was sober to how drunk she was, although there is no basis to think that she was drunk. Then he fills in the ladies and gentlemen of his imaginary jury on all the deleterious effects of drunkenness, including mistaken identity. Maybe this person who accused Kavanaugh confused him with someone else for thirty-five years!

And then, by the end of the statement, he's talking about her drunkenness as though it's been established. It sounds as though he's convinced himself, on the basis of his own testimony out of thin air and a deep commitment to ramming through Kavanaugh's nomination (he supported the nomination in various public ways; the two men worked in the Bush Jr. administration together).

This is a lot for Whelan to imagine about a woman of whom he then knew nothing beyond the summary of a letter she wrote, describing an attack by Kavanaugh at a party. As the *New Yorker* put it, "She claimed in the letter that Kavanaugh and a classmate of his, both of whom had been drinking, turned up music that was playing in the room to conceal the sound of her protests, and that Kavanaugh covered her mouth with his hand. She was able to free herself." The account adds that "the woman said that the memory had been a source of ongoing distress for her, and that she had sought psychological treatment as a result." Since then, Christine Blasey Ford has come forward, telling the *Washington Post*, "I feel like my civic responsibility is outweighing my anguish and terror about retaliation." For the record, "She said that each person had one beer but that Kavanaugh and Judge had started drinking earlier and were heavily intoxicated."

So many things make this tweet about that incident a specimen we could put in the museum of misogyny. The first is an old habit of men of this ilk of asserting that women are not to be believed, but men are. There is a long, brutal tradition of asserting that men are credible but women are not, men are objective, women are subjective. This tweet is a model of how men convince themselves their fantasies and delusions are fact—of what arises from an excess of respect for one's own competence and qualifications. That he's not aware of what he's doing—not aware of his subjectivity—is part of the problem, not in this case alone but in so many like it. In a follow-up tweet he said, "Amazed to see how many people responding furiously to this tweet seem to deny that drunkenness could impair a person's cognitive faculties." He's defending what he wishes they were asserting, rather than what they are, since there's a major difference between quibbling about the nature of drunkenness and about whether some-one was drunk.

It would have been a more exotic specimen if ones just like it weren't swarming out of the woodwork. The day before this iconic tweet, the *New York Times* reported on the allegations about Les Moonves, the now former CEO of CBS:

> "We are going to stay in this meeting until midnight if we need to until we get an agreement that we stand 100 percent behind our C.E.O., and there will be no change in his status," said one board member, William Cohen, a former congressman and senator who was defense secretary under President Bill Clinton, according to directors who heard the remarks and other people who were briefed on them.
>
> Another director, Arnold Kopelson, an 83-year-old produc-er who won a Best Picture Oscar for *Platoon*, was even stronger in his defense of Mr. Moonves, the directors and others said. "I don't care if 30 more women come forward and allege this kind of stuff," Mr. Kopelson said in a meeting soon after the conference call. "Les is our leader and it wouldn't change my opinion of him."

These powerful men are asserting that they can have whatever facts they want and make the ones they don't go away. Indeed, these defenders were organizing meetings behind the back of the board member who is the majority shareholder, Shari Redstone, who took the allegations seriously. They don't care what facts women have, because women's facts can be gotten rid of, and indeed the whole long arc of justice now crashing down that we call #MeToo has been about whether women may be in possession of facts and whether anyone will bother to hear out those facts or believe them, or if, hav-ing believed them, they will allow those facts to have consequences.

Take the report Buzzfeed published the same day as the *New York Times* piece on Moonves's defenders, stating that "a former

Michigan State University athlete alleged in a new lawsuit that she was drugged, raped, and impregnated by disgraced gymnastics doctor Larry Nassar." She told her coach, who told the school's athletic director, and then she told the school's police. The two women were thwarted; the lawsuit asserts "not only did Defendant Michigan State University have knowledge that Defendant Nassar sexually abused and sexually assaulted minors, but that it would also go to great lengths to conceal this conduct." We know that Harvey Weinstein's crimes were known to many in his production company, that they required the cooperation of assistants who lured victims in and then left them alone with Weinstein, that they required lawyers and higher-ups in the firm to negotiate nondisclosure agreements and payoffs, that they required the services of spies to go after women who might talk, that they required an army of accomplices.

Imagine that we were, decades ago, a society that listened to women, and that the careers of Harvey Weinstein, James Toback, Bill Cosby, Les Moonves, Roger Ailes, Bill O'Reilly, Charlie Rose, Matt Lauer, Louis C. K., and so many others had been stopped in their tracks. Hundreds of lives would be better, but also the very news and entertainment world we live in might be different, and better. Jill Filipovic noted, in 2017, "Many of the male journalists who stand accused of sexual harassment were on the forefront of covering the presidential race between Hillary Clinton and Donald Trump." She notes that "these particular men hold deep biases against women who seek power instead of sticking to acquiescent sex-object status" and speculates on how it influenced the election.

Women who work at McDonald's and farmworkers from Florida to California have also been addressing the pervasiveness of sexual harassment and assault, as have California janitors, who went on a hundred-mile march to Sacramento to bear witness to the chronic injustice they've endured. The problem is everywhere.

The high-profile cases give us detailed specimens to examine so we can understand the species, and it's important to recognize how widespread the species is, and how it impacts people who clean offices at night as well as those who write TV scripts by day.

For a long time women who had been sexually assaulted had the facts on their side, but the men who assaulted them and accomplices of those men controlled the narrative, including the business of who would be heard and believed. It's in that light that Whelan's tweet unfolds as a perfect type specimen.

Deep in the narrative of Tara Westover's 2018 book *Educated*, she hits the point where her family—fundamentalist Mormon, semi-survivalist, utterly patriarchal—insists on denying the reality of her brother's horrific serial violence and psychological abuse against her and her sister that everyone in the family has witnessed. The sisters are being asked to destroy their own ability to perceive reality, to distrust their own memory, to surrender the right to decide what is true. The structure of male authority requires the fiction of unbreakable male legitimacy, which requires the denial of what everyone knows. They will be destroyed that a man may be intact, and his right to abuse may be intact, and everyone will be crazy in this system, because they will all be denying what happened. This is the family-scale version of Orwell's "War is peace. Freedom is slavery. Ignorance is strength." Authoritarianism, too, begins at home. When I read Westover's account, it felt shocking, and then I realized that it was an experience many women, myself included, have had, only more clear-cut and extreme.

She writes about the way her memories of her family became "ominous, indicting. . . . This monster child stalked me for a month before I found a logic to banish her: that I was likely insane. If I was insane, everything could be made to make sense. If I was sane nothing could." Apparently "make sense" here means to correspond to the official, acceptable version of her family story. Testimony from other family members—the dissenting minority—and an outside witness, and then another, helped her recognize that she was sane and what she remembered had in fact happened. Her book is about making her own independent sense of it all as she emerged into the larger world from a domestic sphere defined by her father's delusions and fanaticism.

This is the horrible conundrum of our two-faced society: we officially condemn rape and molestation, harassment and abuse, but too many within that "we" have also often insisted that those things did not happen when they did, and this denial is part of the fiction that men are objective, women are subjective, so subjective we must find them crazy, delusional—or maybe drunk at the time and prone to mistaken identity. Westover is one among many who has told us how this system can make women believe this of themselves, even demands it of us.

TV writer Megan Ganz was extensively harassed by her boss, and in January 2018 that boss issued a rare, genuine, extensive apology that included acknowledgment of what he'd done. Ganz said two compelling things about it. One was about "the relief I'd feel just hearing him say these things actually happened. I didn't dream it. I'm not crazy." Another was "it took me years to believe in my talents again," because she had been given duplicitous messages about whether she was genuinely admired for her ability or whether that was part of a come-on. In other words, if we unpack the trauma often described as the effect of abuse, we find in it an undermining of the victim's ability to trust her own perception and capacity, as well as a handicapping of her ability to function in social and professional arenas.

Our society defines truth as a valuable possession, of which some people have inherent ownership and others do not, no matter what has transpired and who's raped or lynched whom and what the evidence might show. The novel *To Kill a Mockingbird* is about whether a Black man may own truth, and the unsatisfactory answer is that if a white man decides to defend him among white men, he can have a small helping. It's also a book about a woman lying about rape, a much harped-upon theme in news, popular culture, and literature. A *New York Times* editorial in late 2018 endorsed Betsy DeVos's gutting of Title IX protections of victims of campus sexual assault by leading with a story about a false rape accusation, though campus rape is, like other kinds of rape, epidemic and false allegations rare. And, of course, the same power structure that will not accept true allegations about powerful and elite white men has often proven all too eager to accept false ones about non-elite Black men.

Men with power magnify other men with power, sometimes by commissioning articles by or in defense of men who've assaulted women and making verbal attacks on those women who were physically attacked or those who spoke up for them, as we've seen recently in various New York publications. The *New York Review of Books'* editor in chief saw fit to give Jian Ghomeshi seven thousand words to weasel around his history of violence and its consequences. Ghomeshi, the former star interviewer of the Canadian Broadcasting Company, lied about his brutal attacks preemptively, as the stories were breaking four years ago—he issued a Facebook screed saying he was being stigmatized as a member of an oppressed minority, people who practice BDSM. But, as actual BDSM practitioners pointed out, consent is fundamental to their sexual activities, and the women who came forward told grim stories of being assaulted suddenly, without warning. The cover of the Ghomeshi issue of the *New York Review of Books* was emblazoned with "The Fall of Men," which is a way to frame the rise of women as an unfortunate thing (and what happened to one man, charged with vicious crimes by many women, as emblematic of all men, which is a rather bleak view of men).

Isaac Chotiner of Slate asked *NYRB* editor Ian Buruma about the charges brought against Ghomeshi, mentioning "punching women against their will." Buruma replied with a series of sentences whose dissociative vagueness suggests a tissue dissolving in a mud puddle. He said, "Those are the allegations, but as we both know, sexual behavior is a many-faceted business. Take something like biting. Biting can be an aggressive or even criminal act. It can also be construed differently in different circumstances. I am not a judge of exactly what he did." "I am not a judge" is supposed to sound reasonable, liberal, but in these sentences it seems to mean, I don't care what the women said; either I am ignorant (ignorance is strength) or I am indifferent. I don't want those facts.

In court they were allegations, and in court Ghomeshi's lawyer ripped into them, because in the legal system we settle not for truth, exactly, but for who can more forcefully argue. Out of court they were stories told by women who were reluctant or fearful to speak up, told to journalists who felt the stories had enough credibility to publish. Many women who did not know each other told stories of the same kind of sudden assault. Ghomeshi lied at the outset; is there a reason to assume that at some point thereafter he became a reliable witness? (It's worth remembering that perpetrators of sexual and gender abuse routinely lie, as most people accused of crimes do.) As Jeet Heer put it in the *New Republic*, "The *New York Review of Books* lets Jian Ghomeshi whitewash his past. . . . Though guaranteed to generate backlash for its personal exculpation marinated in self-pity, the piece's egotistical approach also obscures the facts of the case."

"Until the lion learns how to write, every story will glorify the hunter," says an African proverb. But what if the lionesses write eloquently but the editors prefer the hunters' version? Shutting up lionesses is standard, and so is exonerating hunters. The October 2018 issue of *Harper's* included an essay by former NPR host John Hockenberry, widely accused of harassment. Simultaneously, *New York* magazine published a piece distorting the facts (as described in the custody ruling) of the Woody Allen molestation case and maligning Dylan and Mia Farrow all over again; it was supposed to be a profile of Allen's wife, Soon-Yi Previn, but she became a mouthpiece for Allen's defense and her own interests and personality were little explored. It was stunning to see an article that announced it was going to tell her story turn her into a tool for defending his story and for attacking other women.

The *New York Times* reported on how another hunter went after a lioness: "Jeff Fager, who was only the second person in 50 years to oversee *60 Minutes*, was fired for sending a text message that threatened the career of a CBS reporter, Jericka Duncan, who was looking into allegations of sexual harassment leveled against him and Mr. Moonves." Rebecca Traister wrote, early in the flood of #MeToo stories in 2017, "We see that the men who have had the power to abuse women's bodies and psyches throughout their careers are in many cases also the ones in charge of our political and cultural stories." And those stories were, in both politics and entertainment, centered on men—women in television have described how Moonves shut them out—and on male legitimacy.

Canute the Great, son of Sweyn Forkbeard, King of Norway, Denmark, and England, sits, in the famous fable about him, at the edge of the sea and commands the sea to stop: his point is that he's not actually in charge of the tides, but it might also be read as a story about his being a decent politician who acknowledges the limits of his puissance in the face of the facts. It's easy to imagine an authoritarian who insists that the sea has obeyed him, or, indeed, a president who insists that three thousand people did not die in Puerto Rico, or governments that shush mention that the oceans are rising—as the South Carolina government did, in 2012, by passing a bill that specified "the Coastal Resources Commission and the Division of Coastal Management of the Department of Environment and Natural Resources shall not define rates of sea-level change for regulatory purposes prior to July 1, 2016."

One of the rights that the powerful often assume is the power to dictate reality. As Tara Westover's family did, as Cosby and Moonves and their supporters did. As Karl Rove did in his famous sneer about the "reality-based community" during the height of the Bush administration's power. That was when Brett Kavanaugh, now a Supreme Court justice, was toiling away for the regime that was instigating wars over fictitious weapons of mass destruction and imagining that torture could extract useful information from its victims, rather than acknowledging that torture always tortures the truth, too. (In his 2006 judicial hearing, Kavanaugh denied having had anything to do with the torture programs, but some say he lied then, too.) The current president is seemingly convinced that through sheer insistence and aggression he can dictate reality, and you cannot regard this as mere delusion, because it often does work for these figures. Ignorance is strength.

Canute is great because he's not the emperor whose nonexistent new clothes the courtiers obediently admire. He recognizes that facts are beyond his control. In contrast, Hans Christian Andersen's biting fairy tale is about how people go along with the delusions and denials of the powerful, though in Andersen's story the emperor is a fool, not a conspirator. But in the cases of so many of these men insisting that their colleagues are innocent and their accusers incredible, it's not even new clothes we're supposed to admire but old rags.

Discrediting particular women and constructing narratives in which women are unreliable narrators and men are in charge of the truth are among the emperor's old rags, and I'd like to make a bonfire of them. Until then, I find it useful to collect type specimens, tell the truth to the best of my ability about this horrible tangle, and try to map or machete some paths out of it.

Dear Christine Blasey Ford: You Are a Welcome Earthquake

Dear Dr. Christine Blasey Ford,

I am writing to thank you. No matter how harrowing your experience, no matter what the US Senate does in the weeks to come, you have achieved something profound in its power and impact, something that benefits all of us. For there are two arenas in which your words will reverberate—the Senate, and the immeasurably vast realm of public discourse and societal values. Even if your words, like Anita Hill's, are discounted in the former, they will echo in the latter for a long time to come.

You said at the outset of this ordeal: "I was . . . wondering whether I would just be jumping in front of a train that was headed to where it was headed anyway, and that I would just be personally annihilated." Testifying in front of that audience, made up in no small part of hostile, disbelieving supporters of the man you told them assaulted you, may have felt like annihilation. Going into your deepest trauma in front of the nation must have been a harsh ordeal. But you were not annihilated; you were amplified in all senses of the word.

Sexual assault denies a victim her voice, the right to say no and have it mean anything. Your account of his hand clamped over your mouth makes this experience of being silenced a direct assault. A society that then refuses to hear a survivor, that denies her the ability to testify to her own experience, that creates a pervasive hostility that prevents victims from coming forward, erases her and them and us again. But you had a voice that rang out across the world, and you used it to defend this country against a man not just unfit to be a judge but antithetical to what a judge should be: honest, reliable, calm, evenhanded, respectful of the rights of others. Your voice may have shaken, but your truth went marching on.

Anita Hill lost by one linear measure: she did not prevent Clarence Thomas from being appointed to a position for which he remains manifestly unfit. But what she did achieve was not merely linear; her impact, like her voice, spread in all directions. She prompted a searching national conversation about sexual harassment that was desperately needed and that had consequences that benefited tens or hundreds of millions of women in this country and will benefit the generations to come as they enter the workplace. She made an adjustment in the unequal distribution of power—not so grand an adjustment that the problem was remedied, but a shift that matters.

She did so by being, like you, a steadfast witness to her own experience. Many in the media and some in the Senate maliciously insisted on treating her—but not Thomas—as a subjective, unreliable, perhaps delusional, perhaps vindictive person, yet she could not be dissuaded by them.

As you must know better than most of us from your profession of psychology, credibility—being considered a person who should be believed—is foundational to one's standing as a member of a family, of a university, of a workplace, of a society. Anita Hill's testimony and the Senate response put out in the open how women are stripped of this basic power, right, and equality, or are assumed to be incapable or unworthy of it in the first place.

In the wake of Anita Hill's testimony, a vast collective conversation about workplace harassment opened up. Those who had not experienced it directly—at least those who were willing to hear—learned how pervasive and insidious it is and why women don't report it (even recent statistics show how often the consequences for reporting are punitive). Reporting of such harassment increased dramatically, meaning that far more targeted women were able to recognize their mistreatment or tried to find remedies.

The seldom remembered Civil Rights Act of 1991 was passed "to provide appropriate remedies for intentional discrimination and unlawful harassment in the workplace," especially when employers use "a particular employment practice that causes a disparate impact on the basis of race, color, religion, sex, or national origin." And the next year the federal election became known as "the year of the woman," because more women ran for office and won than ever before. The shockwaves of her testimony rippled outward in all directions.

It is too soon to measure the consequences of your testimony, Dr. Ford, though there have been endless media assertions that this confrontation between you and Judge Kavanaugh was a test of #MeToo (even the headlines put on one of my essays framed it that way). There are so many problems with that framework.

One is that #MeToo is only one fruitful year in a project for the rights and equality of women that goes back more than fifty years by one measure, almost 180 by others. Another is that what all this has sought to change is patriarchy, an institution that is thousands of years old. The test of our success is in the remarkable legal and cultural shifts we have achieved over the past fifty years, not whether or not we have changed everyone and everything in the past year. That we have not changed everything does not diminish that we have changed a lot.

The word "we" raises other questions. There is not a "we" in this situation. There are many. There are those who have engaged with the news, the conversation, and the literature to understand how pervasive the problem of sexual violence and violence against women is. There are those who are survivors of sexual assault and other kinds of gendered violence—and we are legion—who know all this in visceral ways. And there is another "we" that insists on not recognizing the problem, those who have chosen not to listen to the endless supply of stories. This is one of the huge fissures running through this country and society.

"Bravery is contagious," said senator Patrick Leahy at the outset of your testimony. "You sharing your story is going to have a lasting permanent impact . . . We owe you a debt of gratitude." You have opened up space for tens or hundreds of thousands of others to tell stories that need to be told and that others need to hear. Sexual assault thrives on the silence of its victims, and these past weeks have shattered some of those silences. There is a geological term, *punctuated equilibrium*, that proposes that life on Earth evolves not steadily but with long uneventful intervals ruptured by epochal change. Feminism, too, has its punctuated equilibrium, and the responses to the Anita Hill hearing in 1991 and to many ugly events in recent years have been ruptures that changed the social landscape. You are yourself a welcome earthquake.

You have, by telling your own story with wrenching vividness, opened up space for countless voices to be heard, for many to tell their own stories for the first time, for the balance to again shift a little. You did not want this role, but when you felt it necessary you came forward and you spoke. And for that, you are the hero of millions. I hope that despite the threats and attacks, you can feel how significant that is, and that you know that the threats and attacks are happening because what you do matters so much. One of the two women who confronted senator Jeff Flake in the elevator, in the now-famous video, asked him a question about Kavanaugh: "Can he hold the pain of the country and repair it? Because that is the work of justice." It seems clear to many of us that he cannot, and that in some way you already have. I know I speak for millions when I say thank you.

Let This Flood
of Women's Stories
Never Cease

There's a problem with the way feminism moves forward in reaction to breaking news stories. It brings focus to a single predator, a single incident, and people who haven't faced the pervasiveness of misogyny can build stories around it as to why this was an exception, not the rule, or the act by a member of a subcategory we can dismiss or demonize. That Harvey Weinstein was typical of liberals or of Hollywood, or that Roy Moore and Bill O'Reilly were typical of conservatives, that this mass killer with a domestic violence background was typical of veterans or loners or was mentally ill, that case after case is a glitch in the pattern of society, not the pattern itself. But these are the norms, not the aberrations. This is a society still permeated and shaped and limited by misogyny, among other afflictions.

Obviously—as we keep having to reassure them, because even when we're talking about our survival we're supposed to still worry about men feeling comfortable—not all men, but enough to impact virtually all women. And in another way, yes, all men, because we're all warped by living in such a society, and because as has been demonstrated by Kevin Spacey's case and others, though men are nearly always the perpetrators, other men and boys are sometimes the victims. Being groomed to be a predator dehumanizes you, as does being groomed to be prey. We need a denormalization of all that so we can rehumanize ourselves.

Women spend their lives negotiating survival and bodily integrity and humanity in the home, on the streets, in workplaces, at parties, and now on the internet. The stories that have poured forth since the *New Yorker* and *New York Times* broke the long-suppressed stories about Weinstein tells us so. It tells us so in the news about famous women at the hands of famous men, in social media about the experiences of not-so-famous women and the endless hordes of abusers out there, whether we're talking rape, molestation, workplace harassment, or domestic violence.

This seems to be what's produced the shock in a lot of what we are supposed to call "good men," men who assure us they had no part in this. But ignorance is one form of tolerance, whether it's pretending we're in a colorblind society or one in which misogyny is some quaint old thing we've gotten over. It's not doing the work to know how the people around you live, or die, and why. It's ignoring or forgetting that we had this kind of story explosion before, in the 1980s around sexual violence, particularly child abuse; in the wake of Anita Hill's testimony in 1991; after the Steubenville gang rape and New Delhi rape-torture-murder in late 2012; and after the Isla Vista mass shooting in 2014. One sentence I come back to again and again is James Baldwin's: "It is the innocence that constitutes the crime." He's talking about white people in the early 1960s ignoring the violence and destructiveness of racism, their opting out of seeing it.

You can say the same about men who have not bothered to see what is all around us: a country in which a woman is beaten every eleven seconds; in which, as the *New England Journal of Medicine* put it, "domestic violence is the most common cause of nonfatal injury to women in the United States"; in which male partners and former partners are responsible for a third of all murders of women in the US; in which there are hundreds of thousands of rapes a year, and only about 2 percent of rapists do time for their crimes. A world in which Bill Cosby wielded a power that could silence more than 60 women and let his crime spree go unchecked for half a century, in which Weinstein assaulted and harassed more than 109 women who, for the most part, had no recourse until something in the system broke, or changed. A world in which Twitter temporarily shut down Rose McGowan's account for a tweet related to Weinstein that allegedly contained a phone number, but did nothing when alt-right pundit Jack Posobiec tweeted out the workplace address of the woman who reported that Roy Moore sexually exploited her when she was fourteen, just as it has done nothing about so many campaigns of threat against outspoken women.

Because here's a thing you might have forgotten about women being menaced or assaulted or beaten or raped: we think we might be murdered before it's over. I have. There's often a second layer of threat "if you tell." From your assailant or from the people who don't want to hear about what he did and what you need. Patriarchy kills off stories and women to maintain its power. If you're a woman, this stuff shapes you; it scars you, it tells you that you are worthless, no one, voiceless, that this is not a world in which you are safe or equal or free. That your life is something someone else may steal from you, even a complete stranger, just because you're a woman. And that society will look the other way most of the time, or blame you, this society that is itself a system of punishment for being a woman. Silence over these things is its default setting, the silence feminism has been striving to break, and is breaking.

Each individual action may be driven by an individual man's hate or entitlement or both, but those actions are not isolated. Their cumulative effect is to diminish the space in which women move and speak, our access to power in public, private, and professional spheres. Many men may not have perpetrated it directly, but as some have finally discussed, they benefitted from it; it knocked out some of their competition, it dug a Mariana Trench through the playing fields we're always being told are level. Diana Nyad, the world-famous endurance swimmer who revealed that, starting when she was fourteen, her Olympic-champion swim coach began sexually assaulting her, talks about the harm she suffered, the way that it changed who she was, diminished her well-being. She says, "I might have defied ruin, but my young life changed dramatically that day. For me, being silenced was a punishment equal to the molestation." This story: it could be that of dozens of women I know, hundreds or thousands whose stories I've read or heard.

We treat the physical assault and the silencing after as two separate things, but they are the same. Domestic violence and rape are acts that say the victim has no rights, not to self-determination or bodily integrity or dignity. That is a brutal way to be made voiceless, to have no say in your life and fate. Then, to not be believed or to be humiliated or punished or pushed out of your community or your family is to be treated the same way over again. Ronan Farrow exposed the network of spies employed to keep McGowan silent about Weinstein; fellow *New Yorker* writer Emily Nussbaum noted, "If Rose McGowan had told the story of the Mossad spies earlier, everyone would have simply assumed she was nuts."

That's because we tell stories about what's normal, or we're told them, and this level of malevolence from our prominent men is not supposed to be normal, even when we have so many stories confirming that it is. So many women who told stories about men trying to harm them were treated as crazy or as malicious liars, because it's easier to throw a woman under the bus than a culture. The bus rolls forward on a red carpet of women. Trump gets out of the bus and brags about getting away with grabbing women by the pussy and gets elected president less than a month later. He puts in place an administration that starts clear-cutting women's rights, including the rights of victims of sexual assault.

Fox renewed Bill O'Reilly's contract after he settled a sexual harassment claim for $32 million, a payment for silence from the victim that included destroying all the emails that documented what he had done to her. Weinstein's film company kept paying off victims, and the settlements purchased the victims' silence. Fellow straight men in comedy apparently formed a protective wall of silence around Louis C. K., making it clear that the man who kept jerking off at unwilling, nonconsenting, appalled women was more valuable than those women were and would remain more audible.

Until something broke; until journalists went fishing for the stories that had been hidden in plain sight. And the stories poured forth: about publishers, restaurateurs, directors, famous writers, famous artists, famous political organizers. We know these stories. We know how the victim in the 2012 Steubenville rape was harassed and threatened for reporting a rape by her high school peers. Four adults in the school district were indicted for obstructing justice by covering up the crimes. The message was clear: boys matter more than girls, and what boys do to girls doesn't matter. One 2003 investigation reported that 75 percent of women who reported workplace sexual harassment faced retaliation. Punishment for reporting punishment.

What would women's lives be like, what would our roles and accomplishments be, what would our world be, without this terrible punishment that looms over our daily lives? It would surely rearrange who holds power, and how we think of power, which is to say that everyone's life might be different. We would be a different society. We have shifted a little over the past 150 years or so, but since the Civil War, Black people have still been held back; since women got the vote ninety-nine years ago, women of all colors have still been kept out; and, of course, Black women got it both ways. Who would we be if our epics and myths, our directors and media moguls, our presidents, congressmen, chief executive officers, billionaires were not so often white and male? For the men now being exposed controlled the stories—often literally, as radio executives, film directors, heads of university departments. These stories are doors we walk through or doors that slam in our faces.

It is to the credit of Diana Nyad that, despite having a rapist as a coach, she became a great swimmer, to the credit of those Olympic gymnasts on the US team that they won medals despite having a molester as their doctor. But who might they have been, in their personal lives as well as their professional achievements, without the harm inflicted upon them by men who wished to harm them, who regarded harming them as their right and their pleasure? Who might we all have been if our society didn't just normalize but celebrate this punishment and the men who inflict it? Whom have we lost to this violence before we ever knew them, before they ever made their mark on the world?

Half a century after the fact, Tippi Hedren told how Alfred Hitchcock sexually assaulted and harassed her off-camera and punished her on-camera and then told her, "his face red with rage," if she continued rejecting his advances, "I'll ruin your career." Hitchcock, whose desire to punish beautiful women drives many of his films, did his best to do so, even blocking an Oscar nomination for her starring role in his 1964 film *Marnie*. These famous people are not the exceptions but the examples, the public figures we know, playing out the dramas that are happening in schools and offices and churches and political campaigns and families, too.

We live in a world where uncountable numbers of women have had their creative and professional capacity undermined by trauma and threat, by devaluation and exclusion. A world in which women were equally free and encouraged to contribute, in which we lived without this pervasive fear, might be unimaginably different. In the same way, a United States in which people of color did not have their votes increasingly suppressed, in which they did not also face violence and exclusion and denigration, might not just have seen different outcomes in its recent elections but different candidates and issues. The whole fabric of society would be something else. It should be. Because that is what justice would look like, and peace, or at least the foundation on which they could be built.

Rebecca Traister and others have made the important point that we should not mourn the end of the creative lives of the men being outed as predators; we should contemplate the creative contributions we never had, will never know, because their creators were crushed or shut out. When Trump was elected we were told not to normalize authoritarianism and lies, but the losses due to misogyny and racism have been normalized forever. The task has been to denormalize them and break the silence they impose. To make a society in which everyone's story gets told.

This, too, is a war about stories.

The Problem with Sex Is Capitalism

Since the Toronto bloodbath in April 2018, when a man murdered ten pedestrians by plowing a van into a crowd, a lot of pundits have belatedly awoken to the existence of the "incel" (short for involuntary celibate) online subculture, and much has been said about it. Too often, it has been treated as some alien, unfamiliar worldview. It's really just an extreme version of sex under capitalism that we're all familiar with, because it's all around us in everything, everywhere, and has been for a very long time. And maybe the problem with sex is capitalism.

At the bottom of the incel worldview shared by the killer in Toronto are these assumptions: sex is a commodity; accumulation of this commodity enhances a man's status; and every man has a right to accumulation, but women present obstacles to accumulation and are therefore the enemy as well as the commodity. Incels want high-status women, are furious at their own low status, but don't question the system that allocates status and commodifies us all in ways that are painful and dehumanizing.

Entitlement, too, plays a role: if you don't think you're entitled to sex, you might feel sad or lonely or blue about not getting what you want. You wouldn't feel enraged at anyone unless you thought those anyones owed you. It's been noted that some of these men are mentally ill and/or socially marginalized, but that seems only to make them more susceptible to online rage and internalization of a conventional story, taken to extremes. That is, mental illness or social marginalization doesn't cause this worldview.

Rather, it makes them vulnerable to it; the worldview gives form or direction to isolation and incapacity. Many of the rest of us have some degree of immunity, thanks to our access to counternarratives and to loving contact with other human beings, but we are all impacted by the idea that everyone has a market value.

If you regard women as people endowed with certain inalienable rights, then heterosexual sex—as distinct from rape—has to be something two people do together because both of them want to, but this notion of women as people is apparently baffling or objectionable to hordes of men, not just incels.

Women-as-bodies are sex waiting to happen—to men—and women-as-people are annoying gatekeepers getting between men and female bodies, which is why there's a ton of advice about how to trick or overwhelm the gatekeeper. Not just on incel and pick-up artist online forums but as jokey stuff in movies and books, going back to *Les Liaisons Dangereuses* and Casanova's trophy-taking. Seduction is often a euphemism for siege warfare.

It goes back before capitalism, really, this dehumanization that makes sex an activity men exact from women who have no say in the situation. The Trojan War begins when Trojan Paris kidnaps Helen and keeps her as a sex slave. During the war to get Helen back, Achilles captures Queen Briseis and keeps her as a sex slave, after slaying her husband and brothers (and slaying someone's whole family is generally pretty anti-aphrodisiac). His comrade in arms Agamemnon has some sex slaves of his own, including the prophetess Cassandra, cursed by Apollo with the gift of prophesies no one believes for refusing to have sex with him. Read from the point of view of the women, the Trojan War resembles ISIS among the Yazidi.* Which maybe makes it meaningful that the winner of the Nobel Peace Prize in 2018 was, in fact, a former sex slave and champion of human rights for her people, Nadia Murad (who shared the prize with Congolese gynecologist Denis Mukwege, who cofounded the refuge for rape survivors called City of Joy).

Feminism and capitalism are at odds, if under the one women are people and under the other they are property. Despite half a century of feminist reform and revolution, sex is still often understood through the models capitalism provides. Sex is a transaction; men's status is enhanced by racking up transactions, as though they were poker chips. Basketball star Wilt Chamberlain boasted that he'd had sex with 20,000 women in his 1991 memoir (prompting some to do the math: that would be about 1.4 women per day for 40 years). Talk about primitive accumulation! The president of the United States is someone who has regularly attempted to enhance his status by association with commodified women, and his denigration of other women for not fitting the Playmate/Miss Universe template is also well known. This is not marginal; it's central to our culture, and now it's espoused by the president of our country.

Women's status is ambiguous in relation to sexual experience, or perhaps it's just dismal either way: as a commodity you must be desirable, but the results of that desirability—erotic contact—can be regarded as making you used, contaminated, impure, due for punishment. If men acquire in a sexual transaction, women ap-

---

* Starting around 2014, ISIS committed genocide among the Yazidis by killing men and sometimes boys and enslaving thousands of women and girls, often exploiting them sexually; what ISIS and incels share ideologically would be an interesting study.

parently lose. Both being sexual and not being sexual are prone to punishment, and the ideal woman is supposed to be both, neither, and something impossible in between. And often the sex she has is measured not by whether she enjoyed it but whether her partner did; when you're the commodity, you're not the consumer.

This idea of sex as something men get, often by bullying, badgering, tricking, assaulting, or drugging women, is found everywhere. The same week as the Toronto van rampage, Bill Cosby was belatedly found guilty of one of the more than sixty sexual assaults that women have reported. He was accused of giving them pills to render them unconscious or unable to resist. Who wants to have sex with someone who isn't there? A lot of men, apparently, since date-rape drugs are a thing, and so are fraternity-house techniques to get underage women to drink themselves into oblivion. Brock Turner, known as the Stanford rapist, assaulted a woman who was blotted out by alcohol, inert and unable to resist.

Under capitalism, sex might as well be with dead objects, not live collaborators. It is not imagined as something two people do that might be affectionate and playful and collaborative but as something that one person gets. The other person is sometimes hardly recognized as a person, and often her personhood has to get out of the way for this version to be enacted. It's a lonely version of sex. There are cultures that personify objects and see even stones and springs as animate and deserving of respect; ours is one in which even human beings are seen as objects and commodities not deserving of respect. The former envisions a world alive with presences and consciousness; the latter is many forms of deadness and numbness.

Incels are heterosexual men who see this mechanistic, transactional sex from afar and want it at the same time they rage at people who have it. That women might not want to grow intimate with people who hate them and might want to harm them seems not to have occurred to incels as a factor, since they seem bereft of empathy, the capacity to imaginatively enter into what another person is feeling. It hasn't occurred to a lot of other men either, since shortly after an incel in Toronto was accused of being a mass murderer the sympathy started to pour out for him.

At the *New York Times*, columnist Ross Douthat credited a libertarian with this notion: "If we are concerned about the just distribution of property and money, why do we assume that the desire for some sort of sexual redistribution is inherently ridiculous?" Part of what's insane here is that neither the conservative Douthat nor libertarians are at all concerned with the just distribution of property and money, which is often referred to as socialism. Until the property is women, apparently. And then they're happy to contemplate a redistribution that seems to have no more interest in what women want than the warlords dividing up the sex slaves in the Trojan War.

Happily, someone much smarter took this on before the mass death in Toronto. In the *London Review of Books*, Amia Srinivasan wrote: "It is striking, though unsurprising, that while men tend to respond to sexual marginalisation with a sense of entitlement to women's bodies, women who experience sexual marginalisation typically respond with talk not of entitlement but empowerment. Or, insofar as they do speak of entitlement, it is entitlement to respect, not to other people's bodies."

That is, these women who are deemed undesirable question the hierarchy that allots status and sexualization to certain kinds of bodies and denies it to others. They ask that we consider redistributing our values and attention and perhaps even desires. They ask everyone to be kinder and less locked into conventional ideas of who makes a good commodity. They ask us to be less capitalistic.

What's terrifying about incel men is that they seem to think the problem is that they lack sex when, really, what they lack is empathy and compassion and the imagination that goes with those capacities. That's something money can't buy and capitalism won't teach you. The people you love might, but first you have to love them.

On Women's Work and the Myth of the Art Monster

The labor lawyer I know sees her work as an act of solidarity, though she collects a salary for it, and some of the climate organizers I know collect salaries and care about the fate of the world, and the doctors and nurses I know want to make a living and maybe have nice things and do it their way, as do we all, but also want to save lives when they can be saved and comfort the dying and improve their journeys when they can't, and are so passionate about what they do they also do it for free, often, and offer their services and skills as a matter of course in emergencies.

Writing is also work that straddles this divide; we want to plunge into our own depths, and we want to make something beautiful that will change the world, and we hope that it will not only do that but also change it for the better, and if we're lucky we make a living at it. Anyone reading this is almost certainly someone for whom a poem, an essay, or a book has been a life raft onto which they clambered in an emergency. Yet the selfishness of writers is a recurrent motif, one I wish I could tie lead weights to so it would never bob to the surface again.

I liked most of Claire Dederer's *Paris Review* piece, "What Do

We Do with the Art of Monstrous Men?," sent to me by a woman friend, a brilliant and dedicated climate organizer. I liked it until most of the way through, until Dederer reflects on Jenny Offill's idea of the "art monster":

> My plan was to never get married. I was going to be an art monster instead. Women almost never become art monsters because art monsters only concern themselves with art, never mundane things. Nabokov didn't even fold his umbrella. Véra licked his stamps for him. . . . The female writers I know yearn to be more monstrous. They say it in off-hand, ha-ha-ha ways: "I wish I had a wife." What does that mean, really? It means you wish to abandon the tasks of nurturing in order to perform the selfish sacraments of being an artist.

Of course, lots of men who managed the accounting department or designed machine parts or watched TV all day were also selfish and had their wives do lots of things for them; selfishness is not particular to artists—or to men; there is no shortage of examples of selfish women. Maybe there's a special kind of bohemian-dude selfishness, which the idea of the genius—the person who is more special and important than others—encourages.

Rosemary Hill recently wrote about Ida and Augustus John and their awful, early-twentieth-century marriage,

> The bohemian man may have idealised women as muses and models but he was unhampered by bourgeois obligations to be faithful or to earn money, though rarely was he so unconventional as to undertake any housework or childcare. The bohemian woman with children was as much shackled to domesticity as any solicitor's wife, but without the staff a middle-class household would command or the security.

But in my experience, lifestyle bohemianism and creative production are as often enemies as allies.

Is selfishness necessary to art, more than other things? My labor lawyer friend's kids hate that she travels so much, but she does, and her software-engineer husband holds down the fort when she's gone, because you don't actually have to be female to be a primary caregiver or even an equal partner in caregiving. And she's not selfish to earn a living or to care about laborers as well as her spectacularly gracious and charming kids. Here in the Bay Area, stories of the obscene hours worked by a lot of people in tech are old news, and the single mom in my extended family is usually working two or three jobs to keep the kids housed and fed. I'm not sure I know any stay-at-home moms locally.

There is certainly more self involved in art-making, or some kinds of it, in that it is often solitary, usually introspective, and sometimes personal, but that plunge into the depths may be as much about dismantling the blithe vanities of the unexamined life as celebrating yourself. Even though you write out of a deep solitude, you generally write because you want to say something to other people, and you secretly hope it will benefit them in some way, by offering pleasure or new insight into the familiar or visions of the unfamiliar or just descriptions of the world and our psyches that make the world new and strange and worthwhile again.

You make art because you think what you make is good, and good means that it's good for other people, not necessarily pleasant or easy, but leading toward more truth or justice or awareness or reform. I write nonfiction and know a lot of journalists, political writers, and historians, whose efforts tend to be more overtly geared toward changing the world, but I believe this is true of poets, too. This weekend, a friend sent me a Neruda poem to celebrate the king tides—the exceptionally high winter tides we get here—and though it's hard to say the way this might help someone, it helps me to read:

the disdain, the desire of a wave, the green rhythm that from
the hidden bulk lifted up a translucent edifice

Because pleasure is part of what gets us through and helps us
do what we're here to do. Because the political struggle is to protect
the vulnerable and the beautiful, and paying attention to them is
part of the project.

Dederer writes:

> Maybe, as a female writer, you don't kill yourself, or abandon
> your children. But you abandon something, some nurturing
> part of yourself. When you finish a book, what lies littered
> on the ground are small broken things: broken dates, broken
> promises, broken engagements. Also other, more important
> forgettings and failures: children's homework left unchecked,
> parents left untelephoned, spousal sex unhad. Those things
> have to get broken for the book to get written.

Dederer's framework seems to suggest that to be a woman is to
be a mother and daughter and wife, and each of those things means
being endlessly obliged to others. It postulates that creative work
is in conflict with personal life, and men who have epic creative
lives are skipping other stuff that women can't, without—her verbs
crunch with harshness—abandoning, forgetting, failing, breaking.
The idea that you "abandon some nurturing part of yourself" suggests that you can't be kind and supportive and write, and that the
kindness part of women's lives is inevitably onerous.

It's a conservative framework in an essay that looks askance at
political engagement as another form of selfishness—my climate activist friend had sent me these lines from it: "When you're having a
moral feeling, self-congratulation is never far behind. You are setting your emotion in a bed of ethical language, and you are admiring
yourself doing it." But people bent on admiration admire themselves
at least as much for being worldly, libertine, sophisticated in toler-

ating some bit of outrage or for being neutral and disengaged and above the fray; those who like to congratulate themselves find many ways to do it. And self-enhancement is hardly an adequate reason to devote one's life to organizing farmworkers or protecting the Arctic National Wildlife Refuge, to cite two things people I know are doing. Selfishness is what seems to be at stake here, and both being an artist and being an idealist are put forward as selfish acts.

I've produced twenty books without abandoning anything or anyone, to the best of my knowledge. Marital, parental, filial relationships are—I can't believe I'm saying this again—not inherent in the condition of being a woman. I know women writers whose children are long grown, and a lot who didn't have children, and women writers who've figured out how to write and have children (see above: spouse; equality). I even know male writers who are devoted primary caregivers. Lots of people, women and men and nonbinary people, are involved in the needs of people they love and still passionately devoted to their art, or the revolution, or their profession. Also, their work is often how, when they have families, they support them, because the kids may need their homework checked but they absolutely need a house and some food, clothing, and healthcare coverage.

I wrote my climate organizer friend who sent me the piece, a young woman with an enormous conscience:

> Good creative work is nurture. Of what matters most to the author and the world. I mean, as I said in my *Mother of All Questions* essay: Who the hell wishes Virginia Woolf had babies instead of books? This whole idea that women have to be either/or: I reject it. On your behalf too, and your work is kindness writ large across the sky.

Rachel Carson nurtured her great-nephew as well as the truth that pesticides menace us and birds and ecosystems, and through her final book changed the world, making it safer for millions of children.

That is so planetarily nurturing I can hardly describe its reach and its kindness, and the pelicans, herons, and egrets I saw on the marshes this weekend might have been near extinction as species without her work. Maybe Martin Luther King Jr. should've spent more time with his children, but they were among the millions whose lot was improved by the work he helped catalyze, and it was also their future he was looking to. His words and examples still nurture us, as do those of all the bygone heroes we remember.

Writing is work that can hold up its head with all the other kinds of useful work out there in the world, and it is genuinely work. Good writers write from love, for love, and often, somehow, directly or otherwise, for the liberation of all beings, and the kindness in that is immeasurable.

All the Rage

You would think there would be more literature about why men are so angry—the president, the mob in Charlottesville in 2017, the alt-right generally, the bar brawlers, the wife-beaters, the gay-bashers, the mass shooters, the man who got more famous than he anticipated for screaming at a couple of women who were speaking Spanish in a Manhattan restaurant one May day in 2018. Add to this all the high-powered, high-profile men—the #MeToo perpetrators—who have been cruel and degrading to women, and the men who went berserk when the *New York Times* appointed Sarah Jeong to its editorial board, slinging sexualized and racist insults at her because she had dared to make jokes about white people on Twitter (and in April 2019, the loopy rage directed at computer scientist Katie Bouman, when she was widely celebrated for writing the computer code that resulted in the first photographic image of a black hole). Anger is often entangled with entitlement—the assumption, which underlies a lot of the violence in the United States, that one's will should prevail and one's rights outweigh those of others, and none of the good stuff should belong to them.

Male anger is a public safety issue, as well as a force in the ugliest politics and social movements of our time, from the epidemic of domestic violence to mass shootings, and from neo-Nazis to incels.

Because we normalize the behavior of men, and of white men in particular, the fact that a lot of far-right movements, such as the American neo-Nazi terror group Atomwaffen Division, are almost all male is seldom noted. (Michael Kimmel's recent book *Healing from Hate*, which examines male fury in global politics, is among the valuable exceptions.) We have until very recently treated it as inevitable that women should adapt to these outbursts with mace in our purses, self-defense lessons, and limits on our freedom of movement, tiptoeing around men who use their volatility to intimidate and control others. Instead of a theory of male anger, we have a growing literature in essays and, now, books about female anger, a phenomenon in transition.

Rebecca Traister's recent book *Good and Mad* scrutinizes its causes, its repression, and its release in the last half dozen years of feminist action, particularly in response to the treatment of Hillary Clinton in the 2016 election and in the remarkable power shift that women demanded in #MeToo. Soraya Chemaly's *Rage Becomes Her* focuses on the ways in which women's (and, by contrast, men's) emotions are managed, judged, and valued in contemporary North American life, while Brittney Cooper's *Eloquent Rage: A Black Feminist Discovers Her Superpower* is a first-person narrative about power, solidarity, race, gender, and their intersections. These books have arrived at a moment when a lot of women have changed and too many men have not—and some are, in fact, retreating into revved-up misogyny and rage against the erosion of their supremacy. Women no longer obliged to please men may finally be able to express rage, because we're less economically dependent on men than ever before and because feminism has been redefining what's appropriate and acceptable to express. "Gender-role expectations . . . dictate the degree to which we can use anger effectively in personal contexts and to participate in civic and political life," Chemaly notes. "A society that does not respect women's anger is one that does not respect women—not as human beings, thinkers, knowers, active participants, or citizens."

The same feminist transformations that have allowed this outpouring may eventually wear down the causes of our anger. Much of the anger discussed in all these books comes from being thwarted—from the inability to command respect, equality, control over one's body and destiny, or from witnessing the oppression of other women. One of the pitfalls in trying to establish equality is to confuse gaining power with unleashing rage. For all of us, this is the conundrum: How, without idealizing and entrenching anger, can we grant nonwhite people and nonmale people an equal right to feeling and expressing it?

There's a Zen story that I heard long ago, about a samurai who demands that a sage explain heaven and hell to him. The sage replies by asking why he should explain anything to an idiot like the samurai. The latter becomes so enraged in response that he draws his sword and prepares to kill. The sage says, as the blade approaches, "That's hell." The samurai pauses, and realization begins to flood in. The sage says, "That's heaven." It's a story about anger as misery and ignorance, and awareness as the antithesis.

Verbal rage and physical violence are weaknesses. (Here, I think of Jonathan Schell's book on the power of nonviolence, *The Unconquerable World*, which makes the case that even state violence is ultimately weakness, since, as the book's presiding muse, Hannah Arendt, wrote, "power and violence are opposites; where the one rules absolutely, the other is absent . . . therefore to speak of nonviolent power is actually redundant."). Equanimity is one of the key Buddhist virtues, and anger is considered a poison in many Buddhist philosophies. It too often hardens into hate or boils up into violence.

The sage makes clear that the samurai feels lousy when he's about to commit a murder. Angry people are miserable. The sage also shows that the samurai is easily yanked around by what someone else does or says. Easily angered people are easily manipulated.

Yet here in the West, we talk about anger constantly, and we're a lot more like the samurai than the sage. We assume, at least about male anger, that it's an inevitable and normal reaction to unpleasant and insulting things, and that it's powerful. In the summer of 2018, NBC broadcast a video of a man from Nashville flying into a rage after he repeatedly propositioned a woman at a gas station and she turned him down. (Did he think women came to gas stations to get dates, not gas and maybe a soda? Or did he just think that women in general owed him, and he had the right to punish any stranger of that gender for disobedience?) In the footage, the man jumps onto the woman's car, kicks in her windshield, and then assaults her directly. This inability to take no for an answer is far from rare. Since 2014, a Tumblr titled "When Women Refuse" has kept track of "violence inflicted on women who refuse sexual advances." There is no shortage of examples, some of them fatal.

For those whose anger is sanctioned, its display can net rewards—if you want to be part of a system of intimidation and extortion, if you imagine the people you interact with as primarily competitors to be bullied rather than collaborators to be embraced. Some of the most privileged people on earth are raging and roaring their way through life, notably the president and his older white followers whose faces, scrunched in fury, can be seen at his rallies. These crowds are angry, perhaps because the alternative is to be thoughtful about the unfairness and complexity of this time and place and what they demand of us.

Much of what Traister and Chemaly address in their books is a double bind: we live in a world in which there is a good deal for women to object to, including the fact that a lot of men wish to harm and humiliate and subjugate us, but responding to that comes with its own penalties. When a woman shows anger, Chemaly observes, "she automatically violates gender norms. She is met with aversion, perceived as more hostile, irritable, less competent, and unlikeable." But even if, for example, she says quite calmly that gender violence is epidemic, she can still be attacked and characterized as angry, and that anger can be used as a way to discount the evidence in a society that often still expects that women be pleasing and compliant.

A disturbing anecdote that Chemaly tells shows how early in life women are denied the right to be angry and how that leads to a denial of rights. At her daughter's preschool, a boy keeps knocking down the towers that her daughter builds, while the boy's parents justify his aggression and refuse to prevent it. "They sympathized with my daughter's frustration but only to the extent that they sincerely hoped she found a way to feel better," Chemaly writes. "They didn't seem to 'see' that she was angry, nor did they understand that her anger was a demand on their son in direct relation to their own inaction. They were perfectly content to rely on her cooperation in his working through what he wanted to work through, yet they felt no obligation to ask him to do the same." She should adapt to his malicious behavior and learn limits on her agency and value; he should not do any of those things, and so gender roles are reinforced from early on.

All three authors point out that race, as well as gender, sorts out whose anger is tolerated and whose is condemned. Among the Black women Traister interviewed are Black Lives Matter cofounder Alicia Garza and congresswoman Barbara Lee. Lee tells gripping stories about her own birth—in a hospital that nearly let her mother die because of her color—and about her mentor, congresswoman and 1972 presidential candidate Shirley Chisholm. Chemaly talks about the ways conservatives imagined and impugned Michelle

Obama's anger and also reflects on her own family's avoidance of women's pain and anger. She wonders if it was rage that made her mother break all the best dishes by silently hurling them, if it was rage that her grandmother, kidnapped as a teenager by her grandfather, felt about a life in which she had little say.

Traister's book documents moments when women have overturned expectations of silence and compliance in order to bring about change. As well as recent events, she presents vignettes from earlier eras of American history, covering Mary Harris "Mother" Jones and the Industrial Workers of the World; Fannie Peck, who organized "Housewife Leagues" in Detroit; Rosa Parks and her only recently acknowledged, pre–bus boycott feminism; the drag queens and trans women who led the Stonewall Riot but were lost in the legend; and Anita Hill, who faced viciously condescending white men when she testified in Clarence Thomas's confirmation hearing.

Traister portrays these women's motives for standing up in each case as anger, an anger that gave them the energy to do what they did. Yet sometimes it seems that energy might come from something else. Traister quotes Congresswoman Lee saying that, in public, Chisholm would be "so cool, her voice and demeanor tough and strong and boom, boom, boom," even when she was upset. "But get her behind closed doors? She'd let her guard down and acknowledge her pain." Was her pain the same as anger? Or was it something else? In 1964, civil rights activist Fannie Lou Hamer famously said, "I'm sick and tired of being sick and tired," and that, too, seems like something that is not exactly anger—perhaps it was frustration and combat fatigue. Traister quotes Garza as saying that "what is underneath my anger is a deep sadness" and that it breaks her heart "to hear that a woman as visionary as Shirley Chisholm used to cry." Later, Garza tells Traister that the question for us is this: "Are we prepared to try and be the first movement in history that learns how to work through that anger? To not get rid of it, not suppress it, but learn how to get through it together for the sake of what is on the other side?"

What is on the other side is not quite clear, but Garza definitely takes the view of the sage, though she has compassion for the samurai in all of us. Perhaps Cooper is already there. Her book is as much a book about love as it is about anger: self-love and the struggle to find and hold it; love for the many women in her life, as well as for public figures from Ida B. Wells to Audre Lorde to Terry McMillan to Hillary Clinton (all three authors talk about Clinton); and, at least implicitly, a love of justice, of equality, of righting wrongs and telling truths. It is a warm and generous work, and a fierce one. All three books are compendiums of enormous numbers of anecdotes from and about figures in recent American life, but Cooper's is distinct both for its telling, as the author's own journey, and for its—yes—eloquent personal voice, which, between her erudition (she is a professor at Rutgers) and her command of vernacular, is funny, wrenching, pithy, and pointed.

Returning to the fable, it seems the interaction between the samurai and the sage is about many less obvious things than fury and restraint. One of those things is power: If the sage had held the sword and the power of life and death with it, it's easy to imagine his interlocutor would have been less eager to turn to violence, and their interaction would have stopped with the insult. Imagine that an unarmed woman asked the sage the same question and he told her she was stupid and ineligible for enlightenment. Like the samurai, she might resent it, but, unlike him, she might not express that resentment, because she might expect that expressing it would just open her up to other kinds of condemnation.

Or perhaps she would accept his definition of her worthlessness and his right to disparage her, so she wouldn't even be angry, just miserable because she believes in her own inferiority and his authority. This is another kind of hell in which a lot of people reside. Don't think of the warrioress Uma Thurman in the film *Kill Bill*, where she uses a samurai sword to slice off the top of an (Asian woman) adversary's head; think of the actual Uma Thurman, who seemed, before #MeToo, to have long normalized her abuse by director Quentin Tarantino.

Both Chemaly and Traister see Thurman as a counterexample to the more unrestrainedly angry women they describe. When Thurman was asked in October 2017 what she thought about Harvey Weinstein and the #MeToo insurrection, she was reluctant to vent: "I don't have a tidy sound bite for you," she responded, "because I've learned—I am not a child—and I have learned that when I've spoken in anger, I usually regret the way I express myself. So I've been waiting to feel less angry. And when I'm ready, I'll say what I have to say." For Chemaly, this response shows that Thurman was fenced in by inhibitions; she should have spoken out in the moment. "The actress's sense of her own position," Chemaly argues, "reflected the precariousness of women, even powerful women, when they have this anger."

Traister also analyzes that extraordinary footage of a clench-jawed Thurman (who is the daughter of a renowned Buddhist practitioner and scholar, and who perhaps has absorbed some non-Western ideas about the uses and abuses of anger). But she proposes that "sometimes, there is a strategy behind the suppression of rage; in Thurman's case, she was waiting to tell her story in full." Months later, in an interview with the *New York Times*, Thurman did just that, revealing that she considered that Tarantino had subjected her to "dehumanization to the point of death" when he forced her to perform a stunt in an unsafe car and she crashed, leaving her with permanent, painful injuries. Thurman confided that up until that moment most of the abuse she had suffered from Tarantino—including his spitting in her face—"was kind of like a horrible mud wrestle with a very angry brother." The stunt set-up was different, because it wasn't just degrading but nearly fatal. "Personally, it has taken me 47 years to stop calling people who are mean to you 'in love' with you," she reflected. "It took a long time because I think that as little girls we are conditioned to believe that cruelty and love somehow have a connection and that is like the sort of era that we need to evolve out of." That is, women are conditioned to accept abuse, and to accept it as its opposite (and to keep letting boys knock down their towers). The power to define your own experience is one of the powers that matters most.

Thurman impugned the reputation of two powerful men she'd worked with to speak of her own struggle and the plight of women exactly as she wanted to. She waited until she could be considered and effective. Her goal was not just what we call letting off steam—an industrial revolution–era metaphor that casts human beings as engines in which pressure builds up and must be released. Thurman's goal was apparently to tell the truth in a way that had consequences, for the men who mistreated her and for the public at large—and perhaps for participants in the feminist insurrection under way, because stories like hers can fortify other women and the movement for women's rights. That is, perhaps she was after a larger kind of liberation than immediate emotional release.

Anger itself is a catchall term for a lot of overlapping but distinct phenomena. Among them are outrage, indignation, and distress, which are commonly born of empathy for the victims rather than animosity toward the victimizers. These feelings, which may last a lifetime, may not include the temporary physiological reaction that is bodily anger, with rising blood pressure and quickened pulse, tension and often a surge of energy. That reaction is, in the moment, a preparation to respond to danger. It may be useful if you're actually being attacked; when it becomes a chronic state, it turns the body against itself with impacts that can be devastating or even fatal. I have often been struck by how some of the people who have the most grounds for anger seem to have abandoned it, perhaps because it could devour them. These include falsely accused prisoners, farmworker organizers, indigenous rebels, and Black leaders, who are closer to the sage than to the samurai in our story, and who are powerful when it comes to getting things done and moving toward their goals.

I had a formative experience in the mid-1990s, when I was working with activists trying to expose the effects of depleted uranium on people who had been exposed to it in the 1991 Gulf War and at American weapons testing sites. I took two dedicated experts to a radio station, where they and the radio host talked at cross-purposes throughout the interview. My colleagues were driven by love and compassion for the soldiers and the civilians in the US and Iraq exposed to the stuff, and they wanted to talk about the suffering and the solutions. Their interlocutor—who, if he were female, might've been called histrionic, self-involved, and volatile—wasn't really interested; he seemed to be motivated by hatred of the government and kept trying to turn the conversation to indictments of the institutions of power. He missed what his subjects were trying to say as he tried to beat their story into his mold.

Most great activists—from Ida B. Wells to Dolores Huerta to Harvey Milk to Bill McKibben—are motivated by love, first of all. If they are angry, they are angry at what harms the people and phenomena they love, but their urges are primarily protective, not vengeful. Love is essential; anger is perhaps optional.

If I Were a Man

When I was very young, some gay friends of mine threw a cross-dressing party. My boyfriend at the time, with the help of his mother, did so well that a lot of straight men were unnerved; they needed to know that the simpering siren in the tight slip was not compromising their heterosexuality. I was not nearly so convincing as a Rod Stewart-ish man with charcoal five o'clock shadow, and I was a little taken aback to realize that, to me, impersonating a man meant manspreading on the sofa, belching and scratching personal parts, glowering and cursing. There was a sense of not having to please anyone and not having to be likable that was fun, but it wasn't necessarily someone I wanted to be.

I am old enough that girls weren't allowed to wear pants to school until midway through my elementary school education. I remember a local newspaper columnist arguing in a grumpy panic that if women wore trousers gender would vanish, which he saw as a terrifying thing. I have worn jeans and shoes that are good for rough terrain for most of my life, along with lipstick and long hair, and being a woman has let me walk this line between what used to be considered masculine and feminine. But I have wondered from time to time what life would be like if I were a man. By this I don't mean to aspire to or to appropriate the suffering associated with gender dysphoria and the deeper issues around bodies, sexuality, and sense of self that trans people contend with.

I like a lot of things about being a woman, but there are times and ways it's a prison, and sometimes I daydream about being out of that prison. I know that being a man can be a prison in other ways. I know and love a lot of men, straight, bi, and gay, and I see burdens they're saddled with that I'm glad not to carry. There are all the things men are not supposed to do and say and feel; the constant patrol on boys to prevent them from or punish them for doing anything inconsistent with conventions of heterosexual masculinity, those boys for whom, in their formative years, *faggot* and *pussy*—being not straight or not male—are still often the most sneering of epithets.

Back in the 1970s, when some men were figuring out how their own liberation might parallel women's liberation, there was a demonstration at which guys held a banner that said, "Men are more than just success objects." Perhaps, as a girl, I was liberated by expectations that I'd be some variation on a failure. I could rebel by succeeding, while a lot of white middle-class men of my era seemed to rebel by failing, because the expectations had been set so very high for them. That had the upside of more support, sometimes, for their endeavors, but the downside of more pressure and more exacting standards. They were supposed to grow up to be president, or their mother's pride and joy, or their family's sole support, or a hero every day—to somehow do remarkable things; being ordinary, decent, and hardworking was often regarded as not enough. But success was available to them, and that was an advantage—and still is. We still have wild disproportions on those fronts; the *New York Times* reported, in 2015, that "fewer large companies are run by women than by men named John." Among the top firms in the US, "for each woman, there are four [run by] men named John, Robert, William, or James."

Back when my mother was alive and well, I used to joke that my problem was that I was a perfect son. What my mother expected from me was, as far as I could tell, profoundly different from what she expected from her three sons. I used to joke that they were supposed to fix her roof; I was supposed to fix her psyche. She wanted something impossible from me, some combination of best friend, confidante, nurturer, and person she could dump on about anything at any time or just lash out at without consequences—a person who would never disagree or depart or assert her own needs, a person who was not a person, which is what she herself had been trained to be. She lived about twenty miles north of San Francisco, where I've lived since I was eighteen, and I was willing to show up regularly, including holidays, Mother's Day, and her birthday, bring gifts, listen, and be helpful in practical ways, while carrying on with my own life (I'd left home and become financially independent at seventeen). That was not enough, for a daughter.

As it was, she resented the opportunities I had that she felt she had not, and in some ways she saw my career as disrupting my proper role as her caregiver, or as a caregiver generally. I knew that the acceptable escape from being devoted to her was to devote my life to some other people—to get a husband, to have kids—rather than to be unavailable because I was working and living my own life. When I was young, she would recite to me the couplet "A son is a son till he takes him a wife, a daughter is a daughter all of her life." In her expectations was an undertone of: I have sacrificed my life to others; sacrifice yours to me.

I'm not a sacrifice, but my work was a source of conflict for others as well. I started college early, graduated early, went onward to the Graduate School of Journalism at UC Berkeley, where I took a degree just before I turned twenty-three, worked for a magazine, left the magazine, and inadvertently found myself a freelance writer, which is largely how I've earned my living these past three decades. I published a book at thirty, and then another one—about twenty-four, to date.

Early on in my friendship with an older feminist writer who has written many influential books, we used to laugh about the guys we met who were upset that we had published so much. They seemed to feel that they had to be more successful than whomever they were attracted to; that somehow our creative work was an act of aggression or competition. Women don't approach men the same way (though a novelist once told me his ex-wife made him feel like a race horse she was betting on). We joked, "If I knew I was going to meet you, I would have burned the manuscripts." Or, as I'd laugh later, "Do you think this book makes my brain look big?" Boys can be stigmatized as nerds and geeks, but they can't really be too smart. Girls can, and a lot of girls learn to hide their intelligence, or just abandon or devalue or doubt it. Having strong opinions and clear ideas is incompatible with being flatteringly deferential.

What is regarded as confidence in a man is too often viewed as competitiveness in a woman; what is leadership in a man is bossiness in a woman; even the word *bossy*, like *slut* or *nag*, is seldom applied to men (and the 2019 campaign season is a reminder of how gendered positive words like *charismatic* seem to be, too). A few decades ago, I knew a woman who was a world champion martial artist. Her husband's family was disconcerted by the fact that he could not beat her up. They did not suppose he wanted to, but they presumed he was somehow emasculated by not being able to, by the fact that she did not make him feel mighty in this abominable way. He, to his credit, did not seem to give a damn.

As a girl, I would have liked to have my intelligence and intellectual labors regarded as an unmitigated good and as a source of pride, rather than something I had to handle delicately, lest I upset or offend. Success can contain implicit failure for straight women, who are supposed to succeed as women by making men feel godlike in their might. As Virginia Woolf reflected: "Women have served all these centuries as looking glasses possessing the magic and delicious power of reflecting the figure of man at twice its natural size." Which can come to seem something you're obliged to be and they're entitled to see.

I have met a lot of brilliant men whose spouses serve their careers and live in their shadows, and marrying a successful man is still considered the pinnacle of women's achievement in many circles. Some of those women flourished, but not a few seemed diminished by their role as helpmeet and handmaiden, and, if they got divorced, they divorced the identity they'd helped build and maintain and often the affluence that went with it. There have been so many women who stayed at home and raised the kids while men went off on adventures and pursued accomplishments. There still are. These straight men with thriving careers and families—no one asks them how they manage to have it all, because we know: she's how.

Ms. magazine's first issue, in 1972, published a landmark essay titled, "Why I Want a Wife." It's an appalling list of all the things a wife might do for her husband and children, a woman as a sort of self-managed servant. Even recently, one of my best friends told me he's taken aback at the smiles-and-compliments response to his going about in public with his new son, as if taking care of his kid is some sort of optional special credit he's earning. It's as though everything fathers do, economics aside, is bonus; nothing mothers do is enough. This is one of the reasons why a woman might want to be a man (and why choosing to have children can mean something entirely different for a woman than a man, unless she has that still rare thing: a partner whose commitment to the work is truly equal). Were I a man, or had I a woman as a partner, I might have made very different choices about marriage and children.

One often hears statements implying that it's generous of a man to put up with a woman's brilliance or success, though more and more straight couples are negotiating this as more women become principal breadwinners or higher earners (and Leonard Woolf was exemplary in his support for his wife's work, which vastly outshone his own). The phrases sometimes used for men who partner with successful women—*taking it in his stride, not put out by, okay with, dealing with, cool with*—are reminders that female success can be regarded as some kind of burden, intrusion, or inappropriate behavior. If it's difficult for him that she is good, is it easy for him if she's mediocre, and does that make mediocrity safe or even aspirational?

Growing up, I knew that I was supposed to be the audience rather than a participant or the center of attention. Like most women, even after the age when strangers demanded I give them a smile, I've had complete strangers come up to me to unload their theories or stories at considerable length, without offering any room for reciprocity in the conversation, if conversation is the term for this one-way street. We know the reality of this from studies about how boys are called on more in school, grow up to talk more in meetings, and interrupt women more than they interrupt men.

In the 1990s the artist Ann Hamilton gave her students lightweight 4 x 8 sheets of plywood to carry around everywhere they went for a week. The exercise made them conscious of navigating space; they were awkward, forever at risk of bumping into people and things, probably offering up a lot of excuses. Success sometimes seems like that for women, an awkwardly large thing that is assumed to be in other people's way and for which you might need to apologize periodically. What would it feel like to have a success that does not in any way contain failure, that is not awkward or grounds for apology, something that you don't need to downplay, to have power that enhances rather than detracts from your attractiveness? (The very idea that powerlessness is attractive is appalling—and real.)

Hamilton has had a tremendous career, and some of it came from the sheer scale and ambition of her work from the outset, which seemed exceptional when she appeared on the art scene in the late 1980s. I remember all the women art students I met in that era, who made tiny, furtive things that expressed something about their condition, including the lack of room they felt free to occupy. How do you think big when you're supposed to not get in the way, not overstep your welcome, not overshadow or intimidate? Ann wrote to me when I asked about that plywood assignment long ago: "I am still trying to break the habit of apologizing for myself—even though I have little hesitation in asking for help on projects—asking for myself brings out the old, 'Please excuse me.'"

Women older than I am have horrifying stories to tell, and we are not out from under that shadow. Supreme Court justice Ruth Bader Ginsburg says, of her arrival at law school in the 1950s, "The dean then asked each of us in turn to say what we were doing at the law school, occupying a seat that could be held by a man." It's not just trouble at the top: women plumbers, electricians, contractors, and mechanics have told me about being treated as incompetent, intrusive, or both, in their fields.

It isn't hard to find contemporary horror stories of women who can't wedge a word in edgewise at meetings, have their ideas taken up by others, don't get promoted as they might if they were men, get harassed and groped, or, in the white-collar world, not invited to the executive bonding sessions. Workers' stories of sexual harassment and discrimination are so common in Silicon Valley they seem to describe the rule rather than the exception in tech, and the gist of many is that the tech companies tolerate harassment more than they tolerate people who report it.

We still have a long way to go. A young woman enrolled at a women's college told me this summer she was thrilled to be in an intellectual habitat where no shining young men were going to dominate the classroom conversations the way they had in her high school; walking home across campus at 3 a.m. without thinking about safety was another pleasure. (Women do engage in sexual assault, but in numbers that are minute compared to those of men.) Women are targets in the online world, too; in a little experiment on Twitter, the writer Summer Brenner borrowed her brother's profile picture and turned her first name into initials—the harassment she had experienced online dropped to almost nothing. Women may aspire to be men just to be free from persecution by them, and many women have, since George Eliot, Currer Bell (Charlotte Brontë's pseudonym), and George Sand published under ambiguous or male-sounding bylines for the advantages, or rather the lack of disadvantages, therein. Jane Austen published anonymously during her lifetime.

If I were a man . . . I didn't want to be someone else so much as I wanted, from time to time, to be treated as someone else, or left alone as I would be if I were something else. In particular, I've wanted to be able to walk around alone, in cities, on mountains, unmolested. You can't wander lonely as a cloud when you're always checking to see whether you're being followed, or bracing yourself in case the person passing grabs you. I've been insulted, threatened, spat on, attacked, groped, harassed, followed; women I know have been stalked so ferociously they had to go into hiding, sometimes for years; other women I know have been kidnapped, raped, tortured, stabbed, beaten with rocks, left for dead. It impacts on your sense of freedom, to say the least.

A small part of my consciousness is perpetually occupied by these survival questions whenever I'm outdoors alone, though there are a few places I've been—Iceland, Japan, extremely remote wildernesses where bears were the only menace—where I felt I didn't have to think about it. Solitary walking is where a lot of writers—Wordsworth, Rousseau, Thoreau, Gary Snyder—got a lot of their thinking and composing done; I have, too, but it got interrupted both from outside and from this internal monitor, always thinking about my safety. I know that my whiteness tips the balance the other way with this; it lets me go places that a Black person can't, and the short answer to what my life might be like had I been born Black would be: different in nearly every imaginable respect.

There are many stories of people cross-dressing not as self-expression but for practical purposes, just as there are of people of color passing as white. Deborah Sampson and Anna Maria Lane are among the women who fought against the British in the Revolutionary War dressed as men, and more women did the same in the Union Army during the Civil War. George Sand used a man's name to traverse the literary world of nineteenth-century France and then men's clothes to traverse Paris. She wasn't just hiding out from harassment but putting away the treacherous shoes and yards of fabric that made it hard to walk through a city that was rough-surfaced and filthy. She traded in those fragile things for solid boots and sturdy clothes in which she could roam confidently in all weathers and times of day and night, and loved it.

Not a little of the stuff women wore, and still wear, is an impediment and a confinement. Some women evacuating the World Trade Center on September 11 did so barefoot, lacerating their feet, because their shoes impaired their mobility. What is it like to spend a lot of your life in shoes in which you're less steady and swift than the people around you? Some women wear tight clothes that hamper free movement, fragile clothes, clothes you can trip over. These garments can be fun and glamorous, but as an everyday uniform they're often incapacitating.

Gender shapes the spaces—social, conversational, professional, as well as literal—that we are given to occupy. Who we are, I realized as I cocreated an atlas of New York City, is even built into the landscape, in which many things are named after men, few after women, from streets and buildings—Lafayette Street, Madison Avenue, Lincoln Center, Rockefeller Center—to towns—nearby Paterson, Levittown, Morristown. The nomenclature of the city seemed to encourage men to imagine greatness for themselves as generals, captains of industry, presidents, senators. My collaborators and I made a map in which all the subway stops in New York were renamed after the city's great women. Last year, when I discussed it with students at Columbia University (named after Christopher Columbus, of course), a young woman of color remarked that she had slouched all her life; in a city where things were named after people like her, she might stand up straight. Another wondered whether she would be sexually harassed on boulevards named after women. The world is an uneven surface, with plenty to trip on and room to reinvent.

I like being a woman. I love watching and maybe smiling at or talking to kids I run into in parks and grocery stores and anywhere else; I'm confident no one will ever take me for a creep or a kidnapper, and I know that it would be more complicated if I were a man. There are more subtle advantages to the range of expression I'm allowed in my personal relations, including in my close, supportive, emotionally expressive friendships with other women—and, through all my adult life, my friendships with gay men, many of whom who have boldly, festively, brilliantly broken the rules of masculinity and helped me laugh at the gaps between who we are and who we're supposed to be. Liberation is a contagious project, and growing up around people who took apart and reassembled gender helped liberate even a straight woman like me.

So I don't wish I were a man. I just wish we were all free.

II.
Openings

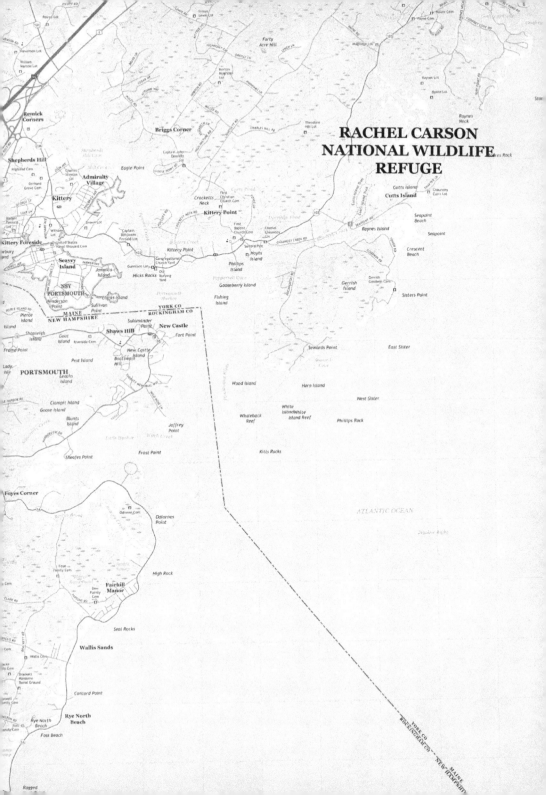

RACHEL CARSON
NATIONAL WILDLIFE
REFUGE

Crossing Over

To *transgress* means to break a law or custom, to go beyond the boundaries or limits, says the dictionary, and then it says that the word traveled from Latin through French to reach English, a nomad word whose original meaning was only to step across or carry across. Borders are forever being crossed; to draw a border is to just demarcate the line across which we will carry dreams, wounds, meanings, bundles of goods, ideas, children. Even the threshold of a doorway can be a liminal space between public and private, between mine and ours; even liminal means a sensory threshold, often in the sense of hovering between states rather than crossing over from one to another.

Transgression is sometimes spatial, but sometimes an act is carried across rules or ideas or assumptions rather than across literal lines and spaces. We have, after all, pain thresholds and ethical boundaries. Sometimes assumptions become transgressions, of at least the truth and sometimes the complexity; sometimes people walk across a landscape on which the lines we know have not yet been drawn. The Spanish conquistador Álvar Núñez Cabeza de Vaca is often described as one of the first white men to reach Texas,

Written to accompany an exhibition of the artist Mona Hatoum's work at the De Menil Collection in Houston in 2017–2018 when he and his companions landed, on makeshift barges and boats made of horsehide, near Houston on the Gulf Coast, after a disaster. Though the histories might as well describe that moment, in 1528, as when the first Black man reached Texas, since Cabeza de Vaca traveled with a Moroccan man described as *negro* in the Spanish narrative. That man is remembered as Estevanico, though that was not his original name, which has been lost to history.

Estevanico was supposed to be Catholic, like all the Spaniards on the expedition that had initially landed in Florida and then stumbled into calamity after calamity, but it is unlikely his conversion was voluntary, likely it was not wholehearted. Estevanico: a Moor, an African, a Muslim captive in Christianity, sent to the Americas, lost in the North American continent, through which he walked for almost a decade. The moment of whiteness and Christianity arriving in Texas was also a moment of Islam and Blackness arriving in a land where both Estevanico and Cabeza de Vaca would be strangers, be enslaved, adapt, become healers and holy men, as they walked across what was not yet conceived of as Texas, on a continent centuries before the United States would be declared, almost three hundred years before anyone would imagine the Rio Grande as a division between nations rather than what a river usually is, a place of confluence of waters and of convergence of drinkers of water.

Estevanico's life was a long series of transgressions, against him and by him, as he crossed through dozens of indigenous territories on his ten-year peregrination through North America. A year or two before the expedition had landed in Florida, a map of the world as Europe then knew it was drawn up by the cartographer Nuño García de Toreno, in Seville; it shows a reasonably accurate eastern coastline of North and South America, studded with a fine, dense lineup of names, like pins or fur, but there is nothing inland, no

Pacific coast for North America, just a long coastline undulating inward at Central America's narrow waist, and then blankness. It is a drawing that depicts that nothing was known to Europe beyond that Atlantic coast. Looking at it now, it's a reminder that the current arrangements—the Europeanization of the Americas, the maps of the world, the assumptions about what belongs where, the places the lines are drawn to delineate borders—arose after this map, that these things are the products of particular conditions, and that conditions will shift again. The truest lines on the map are those between land and water, though with climate change those are due to change; sea-level rise will outdate all the atlases made from de Toreno's time to ours; the other lines on the map are arbitrary and have changed many times and will change again.

The word *Texas* is, like place names across this continent, from Denali to the Yucatan, indigenous, but it wasn't originally the name of a place. It was the word for friends or allies and part of a greeting: *Hello, ally.* The *Handbook of Texas* gives its variations as "tejas, tayshas, texias, thecas?, techan, teysas, techas?" The word got messed with in translation, lost its friendship and its greeting and became attached to a place, though some portion of it lives on in the Spanish-speaking Texans long known as Tejanas and Tejanos, and in Tejano music. *Auia* was the indigenous name Cabeza de Vaca recorded for what is now known as Galveston, after Bernardo Vicente de Gálvez y Madrid.

Cabeza de Vaca and his companions were the very opposite of conquistadors, for the land and the people conquered and transformed them. They were lost; they had little idea where they were; they had no knowledge of the plants and animals, of the languages and customs; they were about as foreign as it was possible to be without leaving the planet. They stepped across, they were carried across, they wandered, and they were transformed as they morphed into something other than the men who had landed. The account Cabeza de Vaca wrote uses the hybrid Spanish-indigenous word *tassajar*, to dry long strips of meat in the sun, to describe what one among them named Esquivel did with another expedition member named Sotomayor, who had perished, and then Sotomayor was carried across the terra incognita as food. At another stage of their arduous journey, they quenched their thirst with the juice of prickly pears, squeezed into a hole in the ground.

The word *metaphor* is more like the word *transgress* than one might think: it traveled from Greek, where it literally means a transfer or a carrying over; it's a word sometimes nowadays written on buses and moving vans there, I've been told. Writing it now makes me think of Syrian refugees sailing to Greece in fragile boats that sometimes sink, of this attempt to carry over from a war zone to an arrival without welcome across the Mediterranean. The word *refugee* comes from, of course, refuge, something that refugees don't always find. Metaphors are transgressive in that they make unalike things alike: in Mona Hatoum's work, a crib is a prison because it also has bars. Bars are test tubes, when they are made of glass. A crib becomes an experimental zone when it's a cage of test tubes; without a baby inside, it can be filled with imaginings.

Metaphors are not how we define territories but how we travel across thresholds between categories. They are bridges across categories and differences. Through them we connect the abstract and the concrete, the small and the large, the live and inanimate, the human and the nonhuman. Sometimes the metaphors are built so deeply into language that we hardly notice the bodily anatomy that gives mountains foothills, rivers headwaters and mouths (curiously, at opposite ends), vases necks, chairs arms, and tables legs. We think through our bodies, and that includes seeing bodies elsewhere, making bodies the terms of understanding how animate and inanimate, tiny and huge objects and systems work. Both needles and storms have eyes. Metaphor is the process of relating things that are alike in some fashion, to some degree, and the literal-minded object on the grounds that there are also differences, while the metaphorically minded understand the limits of similarity.

Country, says the *Oxford English Dictionary*, derives from "Anglo-Norman contré, countré, cuntré, Anglo-Norman and Old French cuntree," and one of its roots—for we describe words as having the roots we know from plants, which suggests they're stable but living—is contra, against, opposite, as in contrary and contradict. In another round of metaphors a living body is a country because a free and equal individual has sovereignty over her body, because both are imagined as clearly defined distinct and separate things, though my body may walk away from yours, yet the United States cannot walk away from Mexico. Bodies are real, while nations are in some sense fictions of separateness, made by drawing fictitious lines on continents (and a few islands, notably the Dominican Republic and Haiti), and then pretending that these are demarcations of true separateness and independence, as though the birds do not fly across the Rio Grande where it is supposed to be an international boundary as readily as they do where it is only the line of muddy water running down the center of New Mexico, as though your arms could declare independence from your chest.

Under patriarchy the ideal body has been imagined as an isolationist nation, an island unto itself, in total control, which makes the female body—or any body whose orifices and interchanges, whose penetrability and vulnerability, are acknowledged—troublesome. Of course, every body is open and porous: five minutes without inhaling the air around you and you're dead; a week without water and you're dry and dead; but it's sexual penetration and penetrability and ideas of openness as erotic and social possibilities that seem to be the source of animosity and anxiety for the men who imagine themselves as islands or fortresses or island fortresses. The many thresholds of women's bodies and what crosses those boundaries has made them endlessly subject to measures to contain and control them, or rather to contain and control the anxiety of a patriarchal society. Patrilineality—the descent of the male line—has also begotten a fury to control women's sexuality, and that fury has for millennia begotten clothing, laws, customs, punishments, architectures, and rules to regulate women's bodies in order to preserve male powers and lineages.

The root of *invade*, from the Latin for *walking in*, connects the word to *transgress* and to *metaphor*. Rape is an act of war, an invasion of an unwilling body to demonstrate power over and to subjugate and punish. There are acts on the scale of nations that impact bodies, and acts upon bodies that impact lives on the scales of nations. Rape has become an even more common, overt tool of war in the past few decades, in Rwanda, in Sudan, and currently in Syria, where the invasion of women's and girls' bodies has become a reason that families leave the country; the threat of invasion leads to the plight of exile. *Occupied territory* is a term that can also be applied to bodies; bodies go into exile to avoid hostile occupation.

In the United States an inverse oppression has arisen with the intensified insistence that some residents here are invaders who should be expelled. The idea of illegal immigrants arises from the idea of the nation as a body whose purity is defiled by foreign bodies, and of its borders as something that can and should be sealed. There is a dream of a nation that is autonomous, uncontaminated, a sort of solid block of impenetrable matter, a dream that defies the reality of circulating air, water, goods, migratory animals, and histories in which other borders or no borders existed, in which most of us crossed many borders to arrive here. It's a fantasy of safety, in which self and other are distinct and the other can be successfully repelled, one that begs and refuses the questions of who *us* is and who *they* are. Isolationism works on both scales.

Isolate, from insulatus, or insula, island. Isolation pretends that parts of the whole are instead autonomous islands, and of course islands themselves are often not isolated at all: they are trading centers, nesting sites for migratory birds, places of coming and going. The rise in pursuit and prosecution of undocumented immigrants has forced many to disappear from public spaces and services. *Harper's* magazine reported in 2017 that there had been a 43 percent decline in the number of Hispanics who reported being raped in Houston. The victims dare not report being sexually invaded for fear of being punished as invaders, here in this nation where 97 percent of rapists already evade conviction in a court of law. *Harper's* also reported that after immigration raids in Las Cruces, in southern New Mexico, elementary school absences increased by 148 percent. Other school districts around the country have had similar withdrawals from education and public life.

Newsweek reported that a pregnant Houston woman, a refugee who arrived long ago, fleeing violence in El Salvador, was making plans to give birth at home for fear of being arrested if she went to a hospital. The fantasy of securing the US–Mexico border and of separating the native-born from the immigrant, the white from the nonwhite, is part of a platform that also includes denying women reproductive rights, which is to say sovereignty over our own bodies. You might think that fantasies of inviolable borders would do the opposite and affirm women's jurisdiction over their own bodies, but, in the battles over reproductive rights, the conservative alignment protects masculine prerogatives by undermining feminine freedom. The nation must be inviolable, its borders secured; the women must be violated, their borders transgressed. Texas now has the highest maternal mortality rate in the developed world, a rate that doubled between 2010 and 2014 (to five times California's maternal mortality rate). The causes include the shuttering of family planning clinics around the state.

Cell, from the Latin for a small room, is in English both the chamber that holds a monastic or a prisoner and the fundamental unit of life, as in *one-celled organism*. Metaphors often work by shifts in scale. Words are artworks, representations, that model analogies and affinities across scales from the cosmological to the microscopic. We grow used to the relationships built into terms like *Milky Way* and cease to see them. There is an art of making things unfamiliar again. "Nobody sees a flower—really—it is so small—we haven't time—and to see takes time. . . . So I said to myself—I'll paint what I see—what the flower is to me, but I'll paint it big and they will be surprised into taking time to look at it," Georgia O'Keeffe once declared.

Much of Hatoum's work operates by shifts of scale that render the familiar unfamiliar; cities, the whole planet, are reduced to the scale of small, two-dimensional cartographic representations, to maps; domestic objects—a grater, an egg slicer—become menacing when they are enlarged to the size of furniture; furniture becomes unfamiliar, the seats of swings are embossed with maps of cities, various beds become objects of discomfort or even torture; hair becomes an ethereal mat, a series of spheres, estranged from the body that produced it. Scale is a form of orientation; changing it generates disorientations that reawaken the eyes and mind. Seeing these works, your own body wakes up to itself; they are visual art, taken in through the eyes but suggesting possibilities and disruptions of body in proximity to them—marbles on the floor to trip on, a grater of a bed that could shred your flesh, cages, swings. You could do things with these artworks; they could do things to you; they place the body in question and sometimes in jeopardy.

Alienate: "To transfer or surrender ownership of (property rights); to make over to another owner. . . . to cause (a person) to feel estranged, hostile, or unsympathetic." *Alien*: "Latin aliēnus (adjective) of or belonging to others, unnatural, unusual, unconnected, separate, of another country, foreign, unrelated, of a different variety or species, unfamiliar, strange, unfriendly, unsympathetic, unfavorable, inappropriate, incompatible, distasteful, repugnant." The wavering lines of coastlines on maps and of hair, on bodies and separated from bodies, conflict with the orderly grids; bars and grids separate and contain some things; others meld and meander and migrate.

Everything in this work is estranged, displaced, uprooted from the habitats of scale and context that make us stop looking. Maybe, as O'Keeffe noted, displacement and attention are related; maybe paying attention is first of all an endeavor to survive and adapt when the unfamiliar arises, startles us out of our habits, carries us over some border into the unexpected. The subtle troubles here, not quite threats but more than ordinary questions, alert us to our condition, our embodiment, our geography, alert us to our own borders and boundaries and what crosses over there, and the ways meaning is always migrant.

Attention, from the French *attendre*, to wait. "Waiting is forbidden," says an enameled metal plaque in the exhibition of Hatoum's work, in Arabic and English. Attention attends, but meaning migrates; wandering and remaining are the measures out of which our lives are made and unmade.

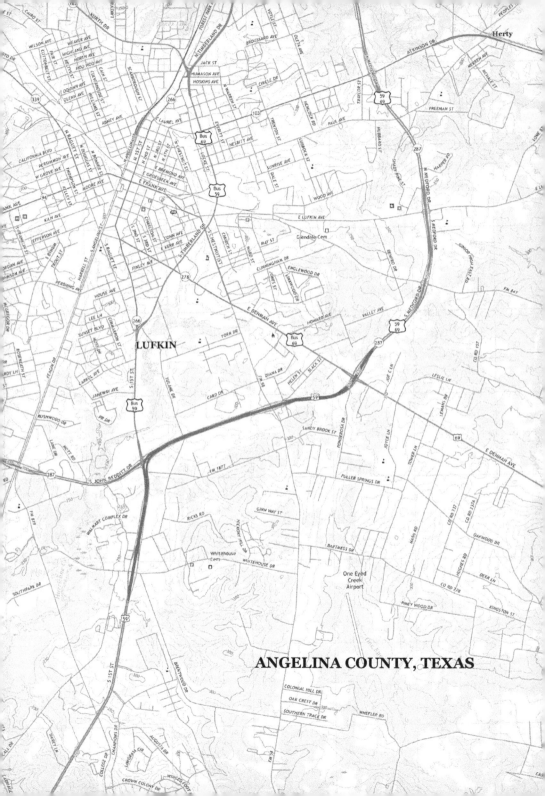

ANGELINA COUNTY, TEXAS

LUFKIN

Herty

City of Women

"It's a Man's Man's Man's World" is a song James Brown recorded in a New York City studio in 1966, and whether you like it or not, you can make the case that he's right. Walking down the city streets, young women get harassed in ways that tell them that this is not their world, their city, their street; that their freedom of movement and association is liable to be undermined at any time; and that a lot of strangers expect obedience and attention from them. "Smile," a man orders you, and that's a concise way to say that he owns you; he's the boss; you do as you're told; your face is there to serve his life, not express your own. He's someone; you're no one.

In a subtler way, names perpetuate the gendering of New York City. Almost every city is full of men's names, names that are markers of who wielded power, who made history, who held fortunes, who was remembered; women are anonymous people who changed fathers' for husbands' names as they married, who lived in private and were comparatively forgotten, with few exceptions. This naming stretches across the continent; the peaks of many western mountains have names that make the ranges sound like the board of directors of old corporations, and very little has been named for

"City of Women" is one of twenty-six maps in the atlas Nonstop Metropolis and is available as a freestanding poster from Haymarket Books.

particular historical women, though Maryland was named after a Queen Mary who never got there.

Just as San Francisco was named after an Italian saint and New Orleans after a French king's brother, the duc d'Orléans, so were New York, city and state, named after King Charles I's brother, the duke of York (later King James II), when the British took over the region from the Dutch. Inside this city and state named for a man, you can board the 6 train at the northern end of the line in Pelham Bay, named after a Mr. Pell, in a borough named for a Swedish man, Jonas Bronck, and ride the train down into Manhattan, which is unusual in the city for retaining an indigenous name (the Bronx is said to have been named Rananchqua by the local Lenape, Keskeskeck by other native groups).** In Manhattan, the 6 travels down Lexington Avenue, parallel to Madison Avenue, named, of course, after president James Madison.

As the train rumbles south under Manhattan's east side, you might disembark at Hunter College, which, although originally a women's college, was named after Thomas Hunter, or ride further to Astor Place, named after plutocrat John Jacob Astor, near Washington Square, named, of course, after the president. Or you might go even farther, to Bleecker Street, named after Anthony Bleecker, who owned farmland there, and emerge on Lafayette Street, named after the Marquis de Lafayette. En route you would have passed the latitudes of Lincoln Center, Columbus Circle, Rockefeller Center, Bryant Park, Penn Station—all on the west side.

A horde of dead men with live identities haunts New York City and almost every city in the Western world. Their names are on the

---

** The North Bronx's Hutchinson River and Hutchinson River Parkway are unusual in that they were named after a woman, Puritan rebel Anne Hutchinson, who became an unwelcome settler killed by the indigenous Siwanoy people there in 1643.

streets, the buildings, the parks, squares, colleges, businesses, and banks, and they are the figures on the monuments. For example, at 59th and Grand Army Plaza, right by the Pulitzer Fountain (for newspaper magnate Joseph Pulitzer), is a pair of golden figures, General William Tecumseh Sherman, on horseback, led by a woman who appears to be Victory, and also a nameless no one in particular. She is someone else's victory.

The biggest statue in the city is a woman, who welcomes everyone and is no one: the Statue of Liberty, with that poem by Emma Lazarus at her feet, the one that few remember calls her "Mother of Exiles." Statues of women are not uncommon, but they're allegories and nobodies, mothers and muses and props but not presidents. There are better temporary memorials, notably Chalk, the public art project that commemorates the anniversary of the 1911 Triangle Shirtwaist Factory fire, in which 146 young seamstresses, mostly immigrants, died. Every March 25 since 2004, Ruth Sergel has coordinated volunteers who fan out through the city to chalk the names of the victims in the places where they lived. But those memories are as frail and fleeting as chalk, not as lasting as street names, bronze statues, the Henry Hudson Bridge building, or the Frick mansion.

A recent essay by Allison Meier notes that there are only five statues of named women in New York City: Joan of Arc, Golda Meir, Gertrude Stein, Eleanor Roosevelt, and Harriet Tubman, the last four added in the past third of a century (since I wrote this, there have been plans to add more, including Billie Holiday and Shirley Chisholm). Until 1984 there was only one, the medieval Joan in Riverside Park, installed in 1915. Before that, only men were commemorated in the statuary of New York City. A few women have been memorialized in relatively recent street names: Cabrini Boulevard, after Frances Xavier Cabrini, the canonized

Italian American nun; Szold Place, after Jewish editor and activist Henrietta Szold; Margaret Corbin Drive, after the female Revolutionary War hero; Bethune Street, after Johanna Bethune, the founder of the orphan asylum; and Margaret Sanger Square, after the patron saint of birth control. Other than Hutchinson River Parkway in the northeast Bronx, no woman's name applies to a long boulevard like Nostrand Avenue in Brooklyn or Frederick Douglass Boulevard in northern Manhattan (though Fulton Street, named after steamboat inventor Robert Fulton, is supposed to be conamed Harriet Ross Tubman Avenue for much of its length, but the name does not appear to be in common usage and is not recognized by Google Maps). No woman is a bridge or a major building, though some may remember that Gertrude Vanderbilt Whitney is the founder for whom the museum is named. New York City is, like most cities, a manscape.

When I watch action movies with female protagonists—from *Crouching Tiger, Hidden Dragon* to *The Hunger Games*, I come out feeling charged-up, superhuman, indomitable. It's like a drug for potency and confidence. Lately I've come to wonder what it would feel like if, instead of seeing a dozen or so such films in my lifetime, I had the option at any moment of seeing several new releases lionizing my gender's superpowers, if lady Bonds and Spiderwomen became the ordinary fare of my entertainment and imagination, or always had been. If you're a man, the theaters are playing dozens of male action-hero films now, and television always has given you a superabundance of champions, from cowboys to detectives, more or less like you, at least when it comes to gender (if not necessarily race and body type and predilection). I can't imagine how I might have conceived of myself and my possibilities if, in my formative years, I had moved through a city where most things were named after women and many or most of the monuments were of powerful, successful, honored women. Of course, these sites only commemorate those who were allowed to hold power and live in public; most American cities are, by their nomenclature, mostly white as well as mostly male. Still, you can imagine.

In the map "City of Women," we tried on what it would look like to live in such power by paying homage to some of the great and significant women of New York City in the places where they lived, worked, competed, went to school, danced, painted, wrote, rebelled, organized, philosophized, taught, and made names for themselves. New York City has had a remarkable history of charismatic women from the beginning, such as seventeenth-century Quaker preacher Hannah Feake Bowne, who is routinely written out of history—even the home in Flushing where she held meetings is often called the John Bowne house. Three of the four female Supreme Court justices have come from the city, and quite a bit of the history of American feminism has unfolded here, from Victoria Woodhull to Shirley Chisholm to the Guerrilla Girls. Not all the subway stations are marked, and many of the women who made valuable contributions might have are forgotten or were never named. Many women were never allowed to be someone; many heroes of any gender live quiet lives. But some rose up; some became visible; and here they are, by the hundreds. This map is their memorial and their celebration.

A Hero Is a Disaster

STEREOTYPES VERSUS STRENGTH IN NUMBERS

For an embodiment of the word *singlehanded* you might turn to the heroine of the recent movie *Woman at War*. It's about an Icelandic eco-saboteur who blows up rural power lines and hides in scenic spots from helicopters hunting her and is pretty good with a bow and arrow. But the most famous and effective eco-sabotage in the island's history was not singlehanded.

In a farming valley on the Laxa River in northern Iceland on August 25, 1970, community members blew up a dam to protect farmland from being flooded. After the dam was dynamited, more than a hundred farmers claimed credit (or responsibility). There were no arrests, and there was no dam, and there were some very positive consequences, including protection of the immediate region and new Icelandic environmental regulations and awareness. It's almost the only story I know of environmental sabotage having a significant impact, and it may be because it expressed the will of the many, not the few.

We are not very good at telling stories about a hundred people doing things or considering that the qualities that matter in saving a valley or changing the world are mostly not physical courage and

athletic violence but the ability to coordinate and inspire and connect with lots of other people and create stories about what could
be and how we get there. Back in 1970, the farmers did produce
a nice explosion, and movies love explosions almost as much as
car chases, but it came at the end of what must have been a lot of
meetings, and movies have not shown a lot of love for community
planning meetings.

Halla, the middle-aged protagonist of *Woman at War*, is also a
choir director, and being good at getting a group to sing in harmony
has more to do with how most environmental battles are actually won
than her solo exertions. The movie—which keeps lingering without
irony on pictures in her Reykjavík flat of negotiations-and-meetings
endurance champions Mohandas Gandhi and Nelson Mandela—
doesn't seem to know it, but it also doesn't seem genuinely interested
in how you do this thing that saves rivers or islands or the Earth.

Positive social change results mostly from connecting more
deeply to the people around you than rising above them, from coordinated rather than solo action. Among the virtues that matter
are those traditionally considered feminine rather than masculine,
more nerd than jock: listening, respect, patience, negotiation, strategic planning, storytelling. But we like our lone and exceptional
heroes, the drama of violence and virtue of muscle, or at least that's
what we get, over and over, and from it we don't get much of a picture of how change actually happens and what our role in it might
be, or how ordinary people matter. "Unhappy the land that needs
heroes" is a line of Bertolt Brecht's I've gone to dozens of times, but
now I'm more inclined to think, pity the land that thinks it needs a
hero, or doesn't know it has lots and what they look like.

Woman at War veers off into another plotline because, after all,
a woman is at the center, and, conventionally, women who do anything impersonal must be conflicted. Like most movies, it's more

interested in personal stuff, or suggests that we do other stuff for purely personal reasons, so the question of what the hell you do about planetary destruction just sort of fades away. It's kind of like *The Hunger Games*, whose author could imagine violently overthrowing an old order—and archer Katniss Everdeen is supremely good at violence—but not creating a new one that's different, or doing anything political with a larger group that's not corrupt and hardly worth the bother. Thus, at the drab end of *The Hunger Games*, Everdeen goes off and has babies with her man in a horribly rugged-individualist *Little House on the Prairie* nuclear-family-in-the-nuclear-ruins way, or if you prefer, a Voltairean "we must all tend our gardens" way, if that's what Voltaire meant at the end of *Candide*. The archer protagonist of *Woman at War* also dwindles down to the domestic in the end, too, to help one person instead of one planet.

I'm interested in impersonal stuff, too, or I'm convinced that this other public and collective stuff that's supposed to be impersonal feeds hearts and souls and is also about love and our deepest needs, because what's deep is also broad. We need hope and purpose and membership in a community beyond the nuclear family. This connection is both personally fulfilling and is also how we get stuff done that needs to be done. Lone hero narratives push one figure into the public eye, but they push everyone else back into private life, or at least passive life.

The legal expert and writer Dahlia Lithwick told me that when she was gearing up to write about the women lawyers who have fought and defeated the Trump administration in civil rights case after case over the past couple of years, various people insisted she should write a book about Ruth Bader Ginsburg instead. There are already books and films (and T-shirts and coffee mugs galore) about Ginsburg, and these were requests to narrow down the focus to one well-known superstar, when Dahlia in her forthcoming book is trying to broaden it to take in under-recognized constellations of other women lawyers.

Which is to say that the problem of the singlehanded hero exists in nonfiction and news and even history (where it was dubbed the "great man theory of history") as much as it does in fiction and film. (There's also a "terrible man theory of history" that, for example, by focusing solely on Trump excuses and ignores the longer history of right-wing destruction and delusion and the host of complicit players in the present.) To concentrate on Ginsburg is to suggest that one transcendently exceptional individual at the apex of power is who matters. To look at these other lawyers is to suggest that power is dispersed and decisions in various courts across the land matter, as do the lawyers who win them and the people who support those lawyers.

This idea that our fate is handed down to us from above is built into so many stories. Even Supreme Court rulings around marriage equality or abortion often reflect shifts in values in the broader society as well as the elections that determine who sits on the court. Those broad shifts are made by the many in acts that often go unrecognized. Even if you only cherish personal life, you have to recognize the public struggles that impact who gets to get married, who gets a living wage and healthcare and education and housing and clean drinking water, and how voting rights or their lack shape these decisions. Also, if you were one of the eighty-two people who burned to death in the Paradise fire in late 2018 or among the Nebraska farmers whose farms went underwater in the unprecedented floods of early 2019, the consequences of public policy were very personal.

We like heroes and stars and their opposites, though I'm not sure who I mean by *we*, except maybe the people in charge of too many of our stories, themselves often elites who believe devoutly in elites, which is what heroes and stars are often presumed to be. There's a scorching song by Liz Phair I think about whenever I think about heroes. She sang:

> He's just a hero in a long line of heroes
> Looking for something attractive to save
> They say he rode in on the back of a pick-up
> And he won't leave town till you remember his name

It's a caustic revision of the hero as an attention-getter, a party-crasher, a fame-seeker, and, at least implicitly, a troublemaker in the guise of a problem-solver. And maybe we as a society are getting tired of heroes, and a lot of us are certainly getting tired of overconfident white men. Even the idea that the solution will be singular and dramatic and in the hands of one person erases that the solutions to problems are often complex and many-faceted and arrived at via negotiations. The solution to climate change is planting trees but also transitioning (rapidly) away from fossil fuels but also implementing energy efficiency and significant design changes but also a dozen more things about soil and agriculture and transportation and how systems work. There is no one solution, but there are many pieces that add up to a solution, or rather to a modulation of the problem of climate change.

Phair is not the first woman to be caustic about heroes. Ursula K. Le Guin writes,

> When she was planning the book that ended up as *Three Guineas*, Virginia Woolf wrote a heading in her notebook, "Glossary"; she had thought of reinventing English according to a new plan, in order to tell a different story. One of the entries in this glossary is heroism, defined as "botulism." And hero, in Woolf's dictionary, is "bottle." The hero as bottle, a stringent reevaluation. I now propose the bottle as hero.

That's from Le Guin's famous 1986 essay "The Carrier Bag Theory of Fiction," which notes that though most of early human food was gathered, and gathering was often women's work, it's hunting that made for dramatic stories. And she argues that though the earliest human/hominid tools have often been thought to be weapons, in all their sharp-and-pointy deadliness, containers— thus her bottle joke—were maybe earlier and as or more important, gender/genital implications intended. Hunting, she notes, is full of singular drama—*with my spear I slayed this bear.* A group of women gathering grain, on the other hand, doesn't have a singular gesture or target or much drama. "I said it was hard to make a gripping tale of how we wrested the wild oats from their husks, I didn't say it was impossible," says Le Guin, toward the end of her essay. Among the Iban people of Borneo, I read recently, the men gained status by headhunting, the women by weaving. Headhunting is more dramatic, but weaving is itself a model for storytelling's integration of parts and materials into a new whole; it is a technology that creates containers and models complexity.

Speaking of women, there's a new drug for postpartum depression (PPD), about which some experts pointed out that

> mothers and advocates alike should consider if the drug is a BandAid on the larger wound of America's treatment of mothers. How would PPD rates be affected if we adopted policies that support parents, like subsidized child care, paid parental leave, and health care norms that center mothers' choices in childbirth and the postpartum period? Pegging the complexities of a new mother's adjustment as a mental illness ignores cultural factors that cause new parents to feel unsupported.

That is, perhaps we need a plethora of acts of kindness and connection, rather than deus ex machina drugs to mute the pain of their absence. (Of course there are drugs that are helpful for mental health, but they are often deployed as alternatives to resolving the conditions that gave rise to mental distress, which can include societal constructs as well as individual circumstances.)

That's another part of our rugged individualism and hero culture, the idea that all problems are personal and they're all soluble by personal responsibility. It's a framework that eliminates the possibility of deeper, broader change or of holding accountable the powerful who create and benefit from the status quo and its myriad forms of harm. The narrative of individual responsibility and change protects stasis, whether it's adapting to inequality or poverty or pollution.

Our largest problems won't be solved by heroes. They'll be solved, if they are, by movements, coalitions, civil society. The climate movement, for example, has been above all a mass effort, and if figures like Bill McKibben stand out—well, he stands out as the cofounder of a global climate action group whose network is in 188 countries and as the guy who keeps saying versions of "The most effective thing you can do about climate as an individual is stop being an individual." And he's often spoken of a book that influenced him early on, *The Pushcart War*, a 1964 children's tale about pushcart vendors organizing to protect their own in a territorial war against truck drivers on the streets of New York. And, plot spoiler, winning.

I was thinking about all this when I was thinking about Sweden's Greta Thunberg, a truly remarkable young woman, someone who has catalyzed climate action across the world. But the focus on her may obscure that many remarkable young people before her have stood up and spoken passionately about climate change. Her words mattered because we responded, and we responded in part because the media elevated her as they had not elevated her predecessors, and they elevated her because somehow climate change has been taken more seriously, climate action has acquired momentum, probably due to the actions of tens of thousands or millions who will not be credited with this change. She began alone, but publicly, not secretly, and that made it possible for her actions to be multiplied by more and more others. I wonder if there's some sort of word that could mean a person and her following as one thing, rather than two.

Thunberg's been nominated for the Nobel Peace Prize, which is sometimes awarded to groups and teams, but awards also tend to single out individuals. Some people use their acceptance speech to try to reverse the hero myth and thank all the people who were with them or describe themselves as members of a tribe or an alliance or a movement. Ada Limón, accepting the National Book Critics Circle Award for poetry in March 2019, said, "We write with all the good ghosts in our corners. I, for one, have never made anything alone, never written a single poem alone," and then listed a lot of people who helped or who mattered or who didn't get to write poetry.

A general is not much without an army, and social change is not even modeled on generals and armies, because the outstanding figures get others to act willingly, not by command. We would do well to call them catalysts rather than leaders. Martin Luther King Jr. was not the civil rights movement and Cesar Chavez was not the farmworker rights movement, and to mistake them for that denies the multitudes the recognition they deserve. More important, it denies us strategic understanding when we need it most. Which begins with our own power and ends with how change works.

In the wake of Robert Mueller's long-awaited report, a lot of people reminded us that counting on Mueller to be the St. George who slew our dirtbag dragon was a way of writing off our own obligation and capacity. Dahlia Lithwick said it best, a month before the investigation wrapped up: "The prevailing ethos seems to be that so long as there is somebody else out there who is capable of Doing Something, the rest of us are free to desist. And for the most part, the person deemed to be Doing Something is Robert Mueller." Leaders beget followers, and followers are people who've surrendered some of their capacities to think and to act. Unfortunate the land whose citizens pass the buck to a hero. One of the arguments for a woman president is that probably no one will see her as a savior who will do it alone.

The standard action movie narrative requires one exceptional person in the foreground, which requires the rest of the characters to be on the spectrum from useless to clueless to wicked, plus a few moderately helpful auxiliary characters. There are not a lot of movies about magnificent collective action, something I noticed when I wrote about what actually happens in sudden catastrophes—fires, floods, heat waves, freak storms, the kinds of calamities that we will see more and more as the age of climate change takes hold. Classic disaster movies begin with a sudden upset in the order of things—the tower becomes a towering inferno, the meteor heads toward Earth, the Earth shakes—and then smooth it all over with a kind of father-knows-best, here-comes-a-hero plotline of rescuing helpless women and subduing vicious men. Patriarchal authority itself is shown as the solution to disasters, or as a sort of drug to make us feel secure despite them.

One of the joys of Liz Phair's song is that she lets us recognize heroism as a disaster itself. I found out, in the research for what became my 2009 book *A Paradise Built in Hell*, that institutional authorities often behave badly in disasters, in part because they assume that the rest of us will behave badly in the power vacuum disasters bring; thus they, too, often turn humanitarian relief into aggressive policing, often in protection of property and the status quo rather than of disaster victims. But ordinary people generally behave magnificently, taking care of each other and improvising rescues and creating the conditions of survival, connecting with each other in ways they might not in everyday life and sometimes finding in that connection something so valuable and meaningful that their stories about who they were, and met, and what they did, shine with joy.

That is, I found in disasters a window onto what so many of us really want and don't get, a need we hardly name or recognize. There are not a lot of movies that can even imagine this profound emotion I think of as *public love*, this sense of meaning, purpose, power, belonging to a community, a society, a city, a movement. I've talked to survivors of 9/11 and Hurricane Katrina, read stories of earlier disasters and blitzes, and found that emotion swimming up through the wreckage and found that people are ravenous for it.

William James wrote, of the 1906 earthquake in San Francisco, "Surely the cutting edge of all our usual misfortunes comes from their character of loneliness." That is, if I lose my home, I'm cast out among those who remain comfortable, but if we all lose our homes in the earthquake, we're in this together. One of my favorite sentences from a 1906 survivor is this: "Then when the dynamite explosions were making the night noisy and keeping everybody awake and anxious, the girls or some of the refugees would start playing the piano, and Billy Delaney and other folks would start singing; so that the place became quite homey and sociable, considering it was on the sidewalk, outside the high school, and the town all around it was on fire."

I don't know what Billy Delaney or the girls sang, or what stories the gatherers Le Guin writes about might have told. But I do have a metaphor, which is itself a kind of carrier bag—and *metaphor* literally means to carry something beyond, carrying being the basic thing language does, language being great nets we weave to hold meaning. Jonathan Jones, an indigenous Wiradjuri/Kamilaroi Australian artist, had an installation—a great infinity-loop figure eight of feathered objects on a curving wall, in the Asia-Pacific Triennial of Contemporary Art in Brisbane—that mimicked a murmuration, one of those great flocks of birds in flight that seems to swell and contract and shift as the myriad individual creatures climb and bank and turn together, not crashing into each other, not drifting apart.

From a distance Jones's objects looked like birds; up close they were traditional tools of stick and stone with feathers attached, tools of making, taking flight. The feathers were given to him by hundreds who responded to the call he put out, a murmuration of gatherers. "I'm interested in this idea of collective thinking," he told a journalist. "How the formation of really beautiful patterns and arrangements in the sky can help us potentially start to understand how we exist in this country, how we operate together, how we can all call ourselves Australians. That we all have our own little ideas which can somehow come together to make something bigger."

What are human murmurations, I wondered? They are, speaking of choruses, in *Horton Hears a Who*, the tiny Whos of Whoville, who find that if every last one of them raises their voice, they become loud enough to save their home. They are a million-and-a-half young people across the globe, on March 15, 2019, protesting climate change; coalitions led by First Nations people, holding back fossil fuel pipelines across Canada; the lawyers and others who converged on airports all over the US on January 29, 2017, to protest the Muslim ban.

They are the hundreds who turned out in Victoria, British Columbia, to protect a mosque during Friday prayers, the week after the shooting in Christchurch, New Zealand. My cousin Jessica was one of them, and she wrote about how deeply moving it was for her: "At the end, when prayers were over, and the mosque was emptying onto the street, it felt like a wedding, a celebration of love and joy. We all shook hands and hugged and spoke kindly to each other—Muslim, Jew, Christian, Sikh, Buddhist, atheist . . ." We don't have enough art to make us see and prize these human murmurations, even when they are all around us, even when they are doing the most important work on Earth.

Long Distance

The present is, by common definition, the instant between the not yet and the already, a moment as narrow and treacherous as a tightrope. But you might instead define it as all that is remembered by those who are currently alive. A version of the now ends when living memory gives way to secondhand memory or recorded history—when the last veteran of a war dies, or a language loses its last fluent speakers. As long as such witnesses are on hand, the now is something bigger than it seems.

Which brings me to Mary Elizabeth Philips, whom I met in 2014, on her ninety-eighth birthday. A lively, gregarious woman, she was born in the South, moved to San Francisco in 1937, lost her first husband when he was killed in the South Pacific during World War II, was happily married twice more and widowed twice more. She had worked throughout her life—by turns as an accountant, an antiques dealer, and a real estate agent. Now, she was being threatened with eviction; an investment corporation had bought her building and was trying to empty it out, one tenant at a time.

On the day of Philips's birthday party, friends and people involved in the housing rights campaign crowded her modest apartment, which was filled with Asian antiques, photographs, and little notes about where household items were located and how they worked. Her neighbor, who wrote the notes and who worked at a public school and was also facing eviction, had told me that Philips liked strawberries, so I brought a strawberry meringue cake and not nearly enough candles. Philips, her hair an ethereal cloud above her animated face, sat in a bamboo chair in the middle of the clutter, reminiscing about the city she had known before the war, a city that I will never visit, though the one I've lived in most of my life is what it became (or, rather, the several cities I've inhabited named San Francisco are its successive generations).

Each era has its own temperament, and one of the joys of listening to Philips was the gaiety and dash with which she spoke. The mood she communicated as she talked about her past—the impression of having met what arose with pluck and humor—was partly hers but partly her whole generation's. Philips laughed when she described telling doctors that she didn't need a smallpox vaccine because she'd survived the disease as a child. She blithely claimed to have met Bonnie and Clyde on a Texas highway during the Depression, recognizing them only later, via a picture in the paper. Wartime blackout curtains, she noted with pleasure, were green on the inside. She met her third husband when his chair collapsed at a party; as he lay flat on his back, she leaned over him and asked, "Do you play bridge?" He did.

Often her anecdotes drifted, as though she were browsing the pages of a disorderly album. On one of my subsequent visits, she was telling me about her habit of lingering with friends in bookstores, when suddenly she remembered a particular book she'd lent someone decades ago and never gotten back. Unprompted, she began to expatiate on its subject: Mary Ellen Pleasant, a Black entrepreneur and abolitionist of the nineteenth century.

Pleasant was an extraordinary figure. She reportedly funded John Brown's raid on Harpers Ferry and, after the Civil War, fought in court to integrate San Francisco streetcars. She was a successful businesswoman at a time when both her race and her gender might have been expected to bar her from such a role, and late in life she was embroiled in scandals with members of the elite white society for whom she acted as a power broker and confidante.

Unsurprisingly, Pleasant was saddled with stereotypes. When she was seen as a deferential servant of whites, she was called a mammy; when seen as a dangerous player in white love affairs and financial dealings, she was a sinister voodoo priestess. Though Philips remembered her as a liberator, the book she had read was a 1953 biography called *Mammy Pleasant*, which indulged both clichés. Because Pleasant was not, as Lynn M. Hudson's more recent biography puts it, a "clubwoman, heroic slave, self-sacrificing mother, devoted wife, or church deaconess," she was excluded from "the canon of acceptable black heroines." Her irreducible complexity, her unfitness for the usual categories of good and evil, meant that she was largely forgotten.

Listening in 2015 to a woman born in 1916 praise a woman born in 1814, I felt acutely the long reach of the present. It seemed, sitting there, that the city we both inhabited was a place full of overlapping gestures, of people looking backward and passing something forward, of the coherence of a storied landscape.

If I was initially startled by Pleasant's appearance in a story told by an old woman about a book she had read half a century ago, I soon realized that Philips's talent lay in stitching the scraps together. In her telling, the city we both inhabited was a place full of overlapping gestures, of people looking backward and passing something forward. Surely something of the present would survive and be loved when it, too, became the past.

There have been many versions of the past as a golden age, attainable only through some brutalization of a minority population, some reassertion of old hierarchies. The Trump campaign's exhortation to "Make America Great Again" is only the most flamboyant of the recent examples. Such ugly sentimentality may make a case against reaching to the past. But it is equally an argument for a present in which people are not so bereft of recent histories that they will accept fictions and oversimplifications of the past. It's an argument for more history, not less.

In the 1990s, the marine biologist Daniel Pauly popularized the term "shifting baselines" to describe the impossibility of accurately appraising the present without a clear sense of the past. A baseline is the stable point from which you measure change in a system before it was damaged or dramatically altered—the usual date on which the spring thaw used to arrive before climate change began, for example, or the total population of a given species before it became endangered. The scientist and filmmaker Randy Olson put it this way:

> If we know the baseline for a degraded ecosystem, we can work to restore it. But if the baseline shifted before we really had a chance to chart it, then we can end up accepting a degraded state as normal—or even as an improvement.

This principle goes far beyond ecology. If history and intergenerational memory give us social and political baselines, amnesia renders us vulnerable to experiencing the present as inevitable, unchangeable, or just inexplicable. There is power and possibility in remembering that booms don't last, that campaigns like those Pleasant supported can alter the fate of a people or even a nation, that the ways in which we think about race, gender, childhood, and age are mutable, that anyone who has lived for more than a few years has lived through violent transformations. Even what we consider the past is not so past. I know people who, as children, knew people born in slavery; they remind me that this atrocity is not so remote that we can discount it.

The tragedy of Philips's eviction was the persecution of an old and frail and exceptionally charming woman, but she was far from the only near-centenarian being forced out; poets, historians, hallowed institutions were being evicted—a Latino drag bar, a downtown watering hole that had survived Prohibition, a historic Black bookstore, thrift stores that had long served the penurious. What replaces these businesses often seems willfully rootless, enterprises that promote visions of a future so sunny the past is lost in shadow. Airbnb, which is headquartered about a mile and a half from Philips's home, has offered landlords and speculators incentives to replace residents of cities (and towns, villiages, and rural communities) around the world with monied transients, to turn larger and larger portions of cities into playgrounds where no one has a baseline for what the place once was and no one is in charge of protecting what it is.

Measured over too short a span, change becomes imperceptible; people mistake today's peculiarities for eternal verities. The image that comes to mind is a map on a phone. When trying to navigate, you see either a picture too small to provide detail or details too close up for context—or you blindly obey orders dictated by an algorithm that has made all your decisions for you, and never fully grasp where you are.

When Emma Morano, the last person certifiably born in the nineteenth century, died at the age of 117, I called my friend Sam Green, who's making a rolling documentary about the regularly changing holders of the title of world's oldest person. He had filmed a number of people born in the nineteenth century; from now on all his subjects will be children of the twentieth. With Morano's passing, the century she'd spent only a few dozen days in finally dropped below the horizon like the setting sun, and what had been the last rays of a fading present became irrevocably past.

The century of Sojourner Truth and Sitting Bull is now entirely out of reach as living human memory and experience, though it still exists at one remove. Morano was born the same year as my grandmother, who died in 1981. Fats Domino is the age of my mother, and still living in New Orleans and carrying on its musical traditions. His grandmother, who delivered him, was born in slavery, sometime before 1863, and lived with him in his childhood. The presence of these survivors of slavery well into the twentieth century is a reminder that, in what we call the prewar era, another prewar, the one we call the antebellum era, was also in the house. The past lives. It broadens the present; it's like turning a tightrope into a boulevard on which you stroll with more stability, with room for more people to pass you, coming and going.

As Sam and I talked about the uses of the past, he began to tell me about his friend, the film scholar and curator Chi-Hui Yang. Several centuries ago, an ancestor of Chi-hui Yang's wrote a generation poem—a traditional poem offering a series of names to be given to successive generations, a set of instructions to posterity. "Before my first child was born, I wrote a letter to ask my father . . . to select a name for my child," it begins, before giving the names, in sequence. David Spalding and his husband, Li Jianhui, who translated the poem for me, explained that its meaning is for the most part straightforward, establishing the family system. The names themselves, however, are less so: "Each one is like a small poem, written in old traditional characters, making translation very difficult."

Yang's family cycled through the lines at the rate of one character per generation. Yang, who belongs to the twenty-eighth generation, shares his generational name, Chi, with his siblings and numerous cousins. It is as though the poem has become a choral piece pronounced so slowly that it takes a millennium to recite it. As though the poem is being said aloud through the lives of each

of those carrying a word of it as name, as though to be an individual was just to be a single character of a poem—not the poem,
the book, the last word, or the first of anything. It implied a sense
of belonging I could hardly imagine, belonging without confining.
Unlike the pedigree of someone I know whose family goes back to
the Norman Conquest, it's not just a claim to a fancy past.

The poem is a living document, and along the way, variations
were introduced: Yang's grandfather added a few words, and, after
many generations of passing on only via sons, Yang's parents gave the
name to a daughter. Still, the tradition remained intact. It communicated a powerful idea of history, of one's place in time, and suggested a sense of belonging and location I could hardly imagine. Yang's
family had the confidence to believe they could embark on a project
across eighty generations, that they could collaborate with people not
yet born, that continuity through unimaginable change was possible.

I am old enough now to be a repository of the way things were
before: I know what it was like before cell phones, before home com-
puters (not to mention the internet), before AIDS, before effective
treatment of AIDS, before the dissolution of the Soviet Union,
before a series of victories for feminism changed women's lives, including mine. The sheer differentness of the past, the reminder that
everything changes, has always felt liberatory to me; to know that
this moment will pass is freeing. There have been, there will be, other ways to be human. But the loss that is not gradual evolution but
eviction and erasure is not liberatory at all.

Mary Elizabeth Philips's eventual victory over her landlords was bit-
tersweet. The owners gambled on her life expectancy and let her stay;
everyone else was forced to go. She died at the end of 2016, secure
in her home but without any immediate neighbors, not long after her
hundredth birthday. And when I last corresponded with Yang, he and

his partner were figuring out how to incorporate the next character of the poem into the name of their daughter, who was born in the summer of 2017.

Recently, I went to visit a row of eucalyptus trees that Philips had mentioned to me, and which I'd been vaguely aware of, and lived perhapds a mile from for thirty years, but never visited. They were planted by Mary Ellen Pleasant, before her death in 1904, in front of what had been the mansard-roofed mansion she shared with a white family with whom her personal and financial relations were ambiguous before they were adversarial. The saplings had put down roots before Japanese immigrants moved to the area, before the mansion was replaced by a medical building, before the Japanese Americans were sent away to internment camps and African Americans fleeing the South took their place, before urban renewal broke up that vibrant Black neighborhood and replaced it with an expressway and boxy housing developments, before so many things.

Mute and enduring, the eucalypti reached across from Pleasant's time to mine. Their longevity seemed to broaden the present, to offer other ideas of what a life span can mean, here in this state where some trees live for millennia and museums hold slices of redwoods labeled with dates going back almost two millennia. You can see Pleasant's trees in a photograph from the 1920s, when they were smaller, shaped like candle flames, dwarfed by the mansion behind them. Nine decades later, the five surviving trees have enormous knobbed bases several feet across that push the sidewalk up into ledges—I tripped over one and nearly fell. Their trunks are wrapped in diagonally peeling shards of cream and gray bark. Far above me, the passing breeze made the sickle-shaped leaves rustle like silk.

Monumental Change
and the Power of Names

In the spring of 2018, New York City removed a statue of racist gynecologist J. Marion Sims from Central Park, and in the fall, the city announced that a statue to Shirley Chisholm, the 1972 presidential candidate who was also the first Black woman to serve in Congress, will be erected in Brooklyn. Before sunrise, on September 14, 2018, San Francisco removed a much-loathed statuary grouping of a Native American man being dominated by a Spanish priest and vaquero. In October, the city renamed the international terminal at San Francisco International Airport after the gay rights leader Harvey Milk. On December 7, the city celebrated that what was once Phelan Avenue (a name connected to the virulent anti-Chinese campaigns of the late nineteenth century) is now Frida Kahlo Way.

Confederate statues have been coming down in many states: a vast monument to victims of lynching opened in Montgomery, Alabama, in the spring; Atlanta renamed Confederate Avenue this fall; and this year a private campaign completed fundraising for a Chicago statue of journalist and civil rights activist Ida B. Wells, born in slavery in 1862. When Baltimore took down Confederate statues on August 16, the city renamed one area the Harriet Tubman Grove, literally switching sides in the Civil War, from pro-slavery Stonewall Jackson and Robert E. Lee to the most famous heroine of the Underground Railroad. Another Tubman statue is going up in Auburn, New York (and the Tubman statue placed in South Boston, in 1999, was that city's first memorial to a woman). Dallas took down a statue of Lee, and New Orleans did the same in 2017, removing four Confederate monuments in all, amid controversy and threats. I never expected to see what I did the first spring afterward: the breathtaking spectacle of the sixty-foot column at the center of New Orleans's Lee Circle without the sixteen-foot-tall statue of the Confederate leader atop it.

Something profound is changing. Statues and names are not in themselves human rights or equal access or a substitute for them. But they are crucial parts of the built environment, ones that tell us who matters and who will be remembered. They furnish our imaginations and shape the sense of the past that we call on to determine what future to choose and whom to value and listen to in the present. That this is all changing signifies several things. Who is meant by "we" is crucial to any place, and a monument that celebrates pioneers or Indian killers—as so many across the West do—classifies Native people as outsiders and enemies. A place that only honors men defines women as nobodies. Colonizers often begin by renaming the places they've arrived in, and decolonization always involves undoing this; victors erect statues to themselves and their version of history. The changing public landscape is not the cause but the result of a deep transformation under way from Alaska to Florida. Not enough or comprehensive or complete—but a beautiful start.

We often talk about such symbols as though their primary impact is on the people they mirror—that the prime beneficiaries of, say, a school named after civil rights leader Rosa Parks would be Black children, and Black girls in particular, but such representation also matters for those who are not Black or female. When you look at white men enraged and indignant at having to share the stage with others, you see the consequences of their formation in a world centered on white men. It's bad for them, too. You can see what's going on in public squares and street names as a rough equivalent to #MeToo and #BlackLivesMatter: a shift in whose voice is heard and whose life valued.

In Canada, starting in 2014, commemorative markers designed by Native artists have been installed at former school sites where indigenous boarding-school students—or, more accurately, prisoners—were abused. Across that nation, more recently, statues of John A. MacDonald have been coming down, because he was not only the nation's founder but also a principal in instituting genocidal programs such as the boarding schools. In the UK, London has added the first statue of a woman to Parliament Square, and Paris is contemplating naming more Metro stations after women (and already added the name of Auschwitz survivor and health minister Simone Veil to the station formerly known as Europe).

Across the Irish Channel, Dublin is a city that has rewritten its past, more cheerfully, since it commemorates not crimes or defeats but its pride in liberation from British colonialism. The city is full of monuments to the heroes and a few heroines of Ireland's liberation and its literature, but the transition was not always gentle. Statues of English kings and colonial administrators were bombed; a mammoth Queen Victoria was dumped from its pedestal and eventually shipped to Australia. In 1966, fifty years after the Easter Rising began the last struggle for Irish independence, a few Irish citizens, in what they dubbed Operation Humpty Dumpty, blew up the huge statue of Admiral Nelson that had long dominated Dublin's central boulevard, O'Connell Street.

The wide thoroughfare that had for a century and a half been Sackville Street, after a colonial administrator, was renamed in 1924 after the man sometimes known as the Emancipator or the Liberator, Daniel O'Connell. Statues of writers are everywhere, though they, too, are mostly men; churches have, curiously enough, been a place where women—as saints and the Mother of God—are most commonly commemorated in names and images, which is why one of the exceptions to the masculinity of North American place names are those of women saints, in Spanish: for example, California's Santa Clara, Santa Rosa, Santa Barbara, and the Santa Ana winds.

It's easy to commemorate the crimes of others in contrast to the heroism of one's own tribe. But Ireland has in recent years been riven by revelations about institutional and clerical sexual abuse of women and children, the virtual incarceration of unmarried pregnant young women in convent-run workhouses, the vastness of their suffering, and their erasure from society while they were alive and after they died. In County Limerick, a monument to children abused in a residential school was installed in 2015; in Dublin, proposals have stalled, despite a recommendation for a memorial in a landmark 2009 report and half a million euros set aside for the purpose.

"A plan to build a memorial in the Garden of Remembrance on Parnell Square in Dublin 1 was refused permission by An Bord Pleanála in November 2013, on the grounds that it would have an adverse impact on the setting, character and function of the existing memorial to those who died fighting for Irish freedom," the *Irish Times* reported, raising the question of whose and what kind of freedoms we commemorate.

In the US, the changing nation is already evident in changing demographics and shifts in the distribution of power. The 115th Democratic caucus in Congress was 39 percent nonwhite—1 percent more than the general population—though the 51 percent of the population that is female is still grossly underrepresented there. The election of two

Native women to Congress in the 2018 midterms was a reminder of the appalling fact that they were the first. But they will not be the last. And it was clear that both Andrew Gillum in Florida and Stacey Abrams in Georgia would have won their respective elections without significant voter suppression. The Republican Party, which willingly jettisoned nonwhites with their politics of white grievance and overt racism, is now hemorrhaging even white women: "We've got to address the suburban women problem, because it's real," said a worried Lindsey Graham in the wake of November's election.

New voices are rising up, and ideas that emerged from the edges are taking their place at the center. Twenty-one young people are suing the federal government over climate change in a suit that should go forward next year, and a fifteen-year-old Swedish girl was one of the most compelling voices at the 2018 climate summit in Poland. Alexandria Ocasio-Cortez's victories were among this year's beautiful surprises, and she brings with her momentum for a Green New Deal that is, among other things, the capacity to imagine and embrace profound change (and that, a poll shows, is embraced by 80 percent of the population). Though the alt-right matters, young people as a whole have more progressive positions on race and sexual orientation, and this summer a Gallup poll suggested that Americans aged eighteen to twenty-nine prefer socialism to capitalism. The shift "represents a 12-point decline in young adults' positive views of capitalism in just the past two years."

That this was a white Protestant nation was a given when I was growing up. But both the whiteness and the religiosity are in decline. The *New York Times* reported, in 2012, "For the first time since researchers began tracking the religious identity of Americans, fewer than half said they were Protestants, a steep decline from 40 years ago when Protestant churches claimed the loyalty of more than two-thirds of the population." In December 2018, a new report in

Newsweek made the profundity of the shift clear: "The median age of white evangelicals is 55. Only 10 percent of Americans under 30 identify as white evangelicals. The exodus of youth is so swift that demographers now predict that evangelicals will likely cease being a major political force in presidential elections by 2024."

This is part of the doom of the Republican Party, unless it morphs into something utterly different—which the other major party seems to be doing, less out of virtue from within than the arrival of new participants from outside. Because even if the percentage of white evangelicals weren't shrinking, the nonwhite population is growing and will be a majority population nationwide in little over a quarter century, as it already is in California. You can see in these name changes and shifts in who and what is commemorated in public places a series of small victories for a more inclusive, egalitarian vision, even in the shadow of the Trump regime—which, in this light, is only a backlash against the inevitability of the end of this era of white male Protestant dominance. Our electoral system is full of built-in advantages for them. The disproportionate clout of small rural states, the electoral college, gerrymandering, and voter suppression keep this new America from expressing itself adequately in elections, though November's huge blue wave swept over many of these obstacles—but these local changes announce that who we are is not who we were.

You can see that it matters in the battles fought over Confederate statues. A number of southern states have passed laws protecting them, yet the city of Memphis found a workaround this year to get rid of statues of Jefferson Davis and KKK founder Nathan Bedford Forrest, and the white riot in Charlottesville in 2017 had as one of its focii the planned removal of a Confederate statue. "You will not replace us," the mob howled, but we will replace their statues, and they can come along or, as the MAGA slogan seems to promise, try to make history roll backward. We can see the conflicts over representation as an unfinished Civil War battle and perhaps a long overdue defeat for the Confederacy.

In Berkeley, an elementary school named after slave owner and racist Joseph LeConte now honors civil rights hero Sylvia Mendez, and the Sierra Club had changed the name of LeConte Lodge in Yosemite a few years earlier (LeConte was also a UC Berkeley scientist and cofounder of the club). In Colorado and Montana, even the names of mountains are being rethought; in Alaska, the highest peak in this country, Mount Denali, got its indigenous name back a few years ago, after almost 120 years of being named after President McKinley, and a statue of McKinley was taken down in Northern California in objection to his racism.

Seeing this extraordinary transformation of the public landscape is seeing that the very ground we stand on, the streets we travel on, and the people we honor are changing. We are laying the foundation for a different place, for a different society, and despite the regressive raging in the centers of power, this widespread process shows no sign of stopping.

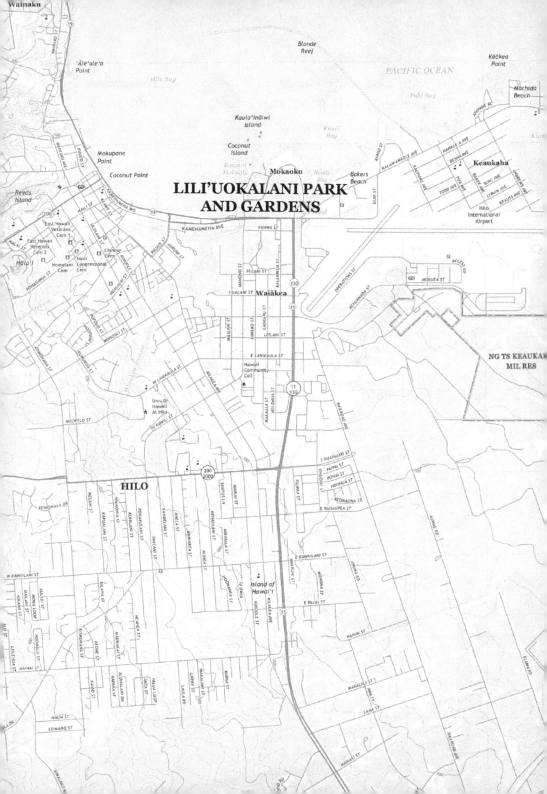

Letter to the March 15, 2019, Climate Strikers

I want to say to all the climate strikers today: thank you so much for being unreasonable. That is, if reasonable means playing by the rules, and the rules are presumed to be guidelines for what is and is not possible, then you may be told that what you are asking for is impossible or unreasonable. Don't listen. Don't stop. Don't let your dreams shrink by one inch. Don't forget that this might be the day and the pivotal year when you rewrite what is possible.

What climate activists are asking for is a profound change in all our energy systems, for leaving fossil fuel in the ground, for taking action adequate to the planet-scale crisis of climate change. And the rules we are so often reminded of by those who aren't ready for change are not the real rules. Because one day last summer a fifteen-year-old girl sat down to stage a one-person climate strike, and a lot of adults would like to tell you that the rules say a fifteen-year-old girl cannot come out of nowhere, alone, and change the world.

Sweden's Greta Thunberg already has.

They will tell you the rules are that those we see in the news and the parliaments and boardrooms hold all the power and you must be nice to them and perhaps they will give you crumbs, or the time of day, or just a door slammed in your face. They will tell you that things can only change in tiny increments by predictable means. They're wrong. Sometimes you don't have to ask for permission, or for anything, because you hold the power and you yourselves decide which way the door swings. Nothing is possible without action; almost anything is when we rise up together, as you are doing today.

I am writing you in gratitude and enthusiasm as someone who has lived for almost six decades, which has been time enough to see extraordinary change. To see what had been declared impossible happen over and over again. To see regimes topple when ordinary people rise up in nonviolent direct action. To see dramatic expansions of rights in both law and imagination. To see what were once radical new ideas about gender and sexual orientation and race, about justice and equality, about nature and ecology become ordinary accepted ideas—and then to see people forget how our minds were changed, and how much that process matters, too.

The world I was born into no longer exists. The role of women has changed extraordinarily since then, largely for the better. The entire Soviet Empire collapsed suddenly, thirty years ago, a few years after the East Bloc of communist countries liberated themselves through the actions of people who were themselves supposed to be powerless to topple regimes backed by great militaries and secret police. I saw apartheid fall in South Africa and a prisoner doing life become its president. I was born into a world where to be gay or lesbian or trans was criminalized, and I watched those laws and attitudes be changed in states, in my country, the US, and in many countries.

I saw wind and solar power go from awkward, ineffectual, expensive technologies only twenty years ago to become the means through which we can leave the age of fossil fuel behind. I have seen a language to recognize the Earth's environmental systems arise in my lifetime, a language that can describe how everything is connected, and how everything has consequences. Through studying what science teaches us about nature and what history teaches us about social forces, I have come to see how beautiful and how powerful are the threads that connect us. Here's one thread. Who did Greta Thunberg describe as a key influence on her actions? Rosa Parks.

That a Black woman born in Tuskegee, Alabama, in 1913 would influence a white girl born in Sweden ninety years later to take direct action about climate change is a reminder that everything is connected and your actions matter even when the results aren't immediate or obvious. The way Rosa Parks broke the rules and lived according to her ideals still matters, still has power, still has influence beyond what she could have imagined, beyond her lifetime, beyond her continent, beyond her particular area of activism.

The rules are the rules of the obvious, the easy assumptions that we know who holds power, we know how change happens, we know what is possible. But the real lesson of history is that change often comes in unpredictable ways; power can suddenly be in the hands of those who appear out of what seems to the rest of us like nowhere. I did not see Thunberg coming, or the Sunrise Movement or Extinction Rebellion or Zero Hour. Good work matters. Acting on your ideals matters. Why it matters is not always obvious and what it achieves is not always immediate or linear.

"I first started considering running for Congress, actually, at Standing Rock in North Dakota," Alexandria Ocasio Cortez said soon after her astonishing 2018 victory made her the youngest woman ever elected to Congress. "It was really from that crucible of activism where I saw people putting their lives on the line … for people they've never met and never known. When I saw that, I knew that I had to do something more."

In 2016, when LaDonna Brave Bull Allard and others launched the camps protesting the Dakota Access pipeline, they could not have known some of the indirect consequences of their actions—including prompting a young woman from New York City to run for office. Today, Ocasio-Cortez represents New York's 14th district in Congress, and more than ninety congresspeople support the Green New Deal that she began promoting after her primary victory in the summer of 2018.

The Sunrise Movement was simultaneously engaged in building awareness and support of the Green New Deal. Founded in 2017, Sunrise is a youth-led movement that aims to "to stop climate change and create millions of good jobs in the process." As the movement's co-founder Varshini Prakash recently told the Huffington Post, Sunrise is trying to "activate the millions of Americans who are ready to fight for a Green New Deal but haven't heard of it yet." For me, the movement's sudden appearance in national politics was even more surprising and thrilling than Ocasio-Cortez's sudden rise to prominence. You never know.

What I see all around me is what I call climate momentum: people from New Zealand to Norway stepping up their response to climate change. I see pipeline blockades in Canada and the US; I see investors backing off from fracking and coal; I see universities and pension funds divesting from fossil fuel; I see solar farms and wind turbines going in all over the world and engineers working to make the technologies better and cheaper; I see lawsuits against oil companies and coal companies; I see politicians, newspaper editorialists, businesspeople, and others who have power under the usual rules getting on board in a way they never have before. There is so much happening, in so many ways, to respond to the biggest disaster our species has ever faced.

It is not yet enough, but it is a sign that more and more are facing the catastrophe and are doing something about it. I don't know what will happen, because what will happen is what we make happen. That is why there's a global climate strike today.

This is why I've started saying, Don't ask what will happen. Be what happens.

Today, you are what is happening. Today, your power will be felt. Today, your action matters. Today, in your individual action, you may stand with a few people or with hundreds, but you stand with billions around the world. Today, you are standing up for people not yet born, and those ghostly billions are with you too. Today, you are the force of possibility that runs through the present like a river through the desert.

Love,
Rebecca

Acknowledgments

This book is, in a sense, transcripts of my side of some conversations with the society around me as it undergoes tumultuous changes, with the changemakers winning some remarkable battles against the forces trying to protect the most malevolent parts of the status quo as it crumbles anyway. It's a book that comes out of the seismic activity in feminism, racial justice, climate action, and other human rights movements, out of the way it's changing the public landscape right down to street names and breaking old frameworks.

And that resistance deserves thanks first. Thank you feminism, thank you immigrant rights groups, thank you queer culture, thank you Black Lives Matter and police watchdogs and the lawyers filing lawsuits on behalf of the vulnerable, thank you fellow marchers in the street and resistance camp residents and all the people who made the 2018 blue wave that brought an unprecedented number of women of color to Congress, thank you voting rights activists, thank you to the innumerable reporters, journalists, editorial writers, and essayists whose work informs mine, thank you to the defense of facts and accuracy. Thank you climate activists—350.org as usual, Oil Change International, on whose board I'm proud to serve, Sunrise Movement, Greta Thunberg, indigenous pipeline blockers, Standing Rock, Green New Deal, thank you to countless local activists and actions, from Jen Castle and Blake Spalding of Hell's Backbone Grill, fighting the Trump administration in Utah, to the people dogging every pipeline and pushing every good piece of legislation and making the news.

And thank you to the editors with whom I worked on many of these pieces, especially Amana Fontanella-Khan and Charlotte Northedge at the *Guardian* (and behind them Katherine Viner); Jonny Diamond and John Freeman at Lithub; and Emily Cook and Katia Bachko, my last editors at *Harper's*; and Chris Beha, who brought me in years before to become the first woman to regularly write the "Easy Chair" column (begun in 1851) there. And to Niels Hooper at University of California Press, where "City of Women" originally appeared as part of our 2016 New York atlas, and to Michelle White of the De Menil Collection, who invited me to write about Mona Hatoum in the essay included here.

Many thanks to Haymarket, whose team—Anthony Arnove, Caroline Luft, Jesus Ramos, Jim Plank, Rachel Cohen—have been a joy to work with over and over again: this is my sixth book with this small, powerful, ideals-driven press. And to my agent, Frances Coady.

And to Erica Chenoweth and L. A. Kauffmann, whose analysis of this moment has been particularly helpful for me; to Taj James for never losing sight of the poetry in politics; to Jaime Cortez for double shots of faith; to Sam Green for cheer; to Ocean Vuong for reminding me that every word matters; to Elena Acevedo and Dahlia Lithwick for perspective and fire; to Conchita Lozano and family for many joint marches in San Francisco's streets; to Chi-Hui Yang for trusting me with his beautiful story, and David Spalding and Li Jianhui for translating it; to Mary Elizabeth Philips for keeping the faith. To the people changing words, from our terms for the climate crisis to the names of streets and schools to the coiners of the new terms that let us describe new things in new ways; to Kimberlé Crenshaw for *intersectional*, which to my geographical imagination always brings to mind actual intersections of city streets; to Daniel Pauly for *shifting baselines;* and to Chip Ward, whose term *the tyranny of the quantifiable* I quote too often.

And to the young ones who give me hope and the really young ones who bring me joy.

Permissions

Previous versions of these essays appeared in the following publications:

"Whose Story (and Country) Is This?" appeared in *Literary Hub*, April 18, 2018.

"Nobody Knows" appeared in the March 2018 issue of *Harper's*.

"They Think They Can Bully the Truth" appeared in *Literary Hub*, July 17, 2018.

"Unconscious Bias Is Running for President" appeared in *Literary Hub*, April 30, 2019.

"Voter Suppression Begins at Home" appeared in the *Guardian*, November 19, 2018.

"Lies Become Laws" appeared in the *Guardian*, June 3, 2019.

"The Fall of Men Has Been Greatly Exaggerated" appeared in *Literary Hub*, September 17, 2018.

"Let This Flood of Women's Stories Never Cease" appeared in *Literary Hub*, November 14, 2017.

"Dear Christine Blasey Ford: You Are a Welcome Earthquake" appeared in the *Guardian*, October 1, 2018.

"The Problem with Sex Is Capitalism" appeared in the *Guardian*, May 12, 2018.

"Women's Work and the Myth of the Art Monster" appeared in *Literary Hub*, December 12, 2017.

"City of Women" is reprinted courtesy of the University of California Press.

"All the Rage" appeared in the *New Republic*, September 24, 2018.

"If I Were a Man" appeared in the *Guardian*, August 26, 2017.

"Crossing Over" appeared in *Terra Infirma: Mona Hatoum*, published by the Menil Collection, Houston, distributed by Yale University Press.

"Long Distance" appeared as "Now and Then" in the September 2017 issue of *Harper's*.

"Monumental Change and the Power of Names" appeared in *Literary Hub*, September 26, 2018.

"Letter to the March 15, 2019, Climate Strikers" appeared in the *Guardian*, March 15, 2019.

About Haymarket Books

Haymarket Books is a radical, independent, nonprofit book publisher based in Chicago.

Our mission is to publish books that contribute to struggles for social and economic justice. We strive to make our books a vibrant and organic part of social movements and the education and development of a critical, engaged, international left.

We take inspiration and courage from our namesakes, the Haymarket martyrs, who gave their lives fighting for a better world. Their 1886 struggle for the eight-hour day—which gave us May Day, the international workers' holiday—reminds workers around the world that ordinary people can organize and struggle for their own liberation. These struggles continue today across the globe—struggles against oppression, exploitation, poverty, and war.

Since our founding in 2001, Haymarket Books has published more than five hundred titles. Radically independent, we seek to drive a wedge into the risk-averse world of corporate book publishing. Our authors include Noam Chomsky, Arundhati Roy, Rebecca Solnit, Angela Y. Davis, Howard Zinn, Amy Goodman, Wallace Shawn, Mike Davis, Winona LaDuke, Ilan Pappé, Richard Wolff, Dave Zirin, Keeanga-Yamahtta Taylor, Nick Turse, Dahr Jamail, David Barsamian, Elizabeth Laird, Amira Hass, Mark Steel, Avi Lewis, Naomi Klein, and Neil Davidson. We are also the trade publishers of the acclaimed Historical Materialism Book Series and of Dispatch Books.

About the Author

© ADRIAN MENDOZA

Writer, historian, and activist Rebecca Solnit is the author of more than twenty books on feminism, western and urban history, popular power, social change and insurrection, wandering and walking, hope and disaster. Her 2018 Haymarket book, *Call Them by Their True Names*, was longlisted for the National Book Award and won the Kirkus Prize for Nonfiction. Earlier books include a trilogy of atlases and *The Mother of All Questions*; *Hope in the Dark*; *Men Explain Things to Me*; *The Faraway Nearby*; *A Paradise Built in Hell: The Extraordinary Communities that Arise in Disaster*; *A Field Guide to Getting Lost*; *Wanderlust: A History of Walking*; and *River of Shadows, Eadweard Muybridge and the Technological Wild West*. A product of the California public education system from kindergarten to graduate school, she writes regularly for the *Guardian* and Lithub and serves on the board of the climate-action group Oil Change International.

CPSIA information can be obtained
at www.ICGtesting.com
Printed in the USA
LVHW091508030120
642454LV00007B/124/P